167

168

dress without any off-cuts or fabric waste. 'Using vintage finds reduces textile waste, but so can conscientious workmanship,' Dornan says. 'Fabric can be draped and cut in an efficient, economical way that minimizes off-cuts, and hence waste. Digital design processes and digital printing use fewer resources than traditional methods.'

Each of Dornan's designs balances luxury and economy, and fuses elegance with understated beauty. Although Dornan never set out to establish sustainable fashion labels, her approach to textile design and initiatives to minimize waste have created exemplary methods of conserving resources without compromising appearance, colour or style.

ABOVE / Dornan's textile designs are used in a wide range of applications. Printed onto interior textiles, they make striking upholstery and eye-catching lampshades. Mounted on stretcher strips, they add an artistic element to the interior.

RIGHT / Earth tones are often combined with colours from nature to create colourways that are soothing to the eye, yet energetic and uplifting too.

ABOVE / Some of Dornan's prints can be described in terms of their romanticism and mystery. This motif, with its floral print and dark background, reveals a neo-Gothic dimension to her work.

RIGHT / Dornan strives to achieve a balance between print design, functionality, texture and colour. Whether adapting a vintage textile for use today or creating a new design for her collection, sustainable principles underpin her work.

Helen Storey's designs are not always made to wear. The fabrics she develops are meant to spark discussions about the environmental impact of the fashion industry, and they do.

131 / HELEN STOREY

ALL IMAGES / Storey merged textile technology with science and biology to explore how clothing could be used as catalytic filters to purify air. The garments are coated with photocatalysts, networks of electrons that break down airborne pollutants into substances that aren't harmful, finding a new use for conventional catalytic convertor technology.

130 / SUSTAINABILITY

LEFT & BOTTOM / Flint's Leaf Wrap prints were made using stalks cut from rose bushes. The bundles were wrapped in fabric and processed to extract the green pigments from the leaves. Flint sprinkled small fragments of iron among the leaves to create a chemical change that created the purple colours.

BELOW / Several different types of eucalyptus plants feature in Flint's work. Leaves, bark and flowers from *Eucalyptus Globulus, Eucalyptus Sideroxylon* and *Eucalyptus Citriodora* are used to create browns, pinks and purples, while leaves from the *Eucalyptus Cinerea* create the rich red colours shown here.

141 / INDIA FLINT

ABOVE / Lupins have orchid-like blossoms. They resemble ornamental plants but grow like wildflowers. Flint extracts dyes from the flowers and freezes them before adding them to the dye bath. The motifs shown here were made by lupin leaves.

FASHION PRINT DESIGN
from idea to final print

FASHION PRINT DESIGN
from idea to final print

Ángel Fernández

4880 Lower Valley Road • Atglen, PA 19310

COPYRIGHT © 2014 BY Schiffer Publishing Ltd.

LIBRARY OF CONGRESS CONTROL NUMBER: 2014940378

All rights reserved. No part of this work may be reproduced or used in any form or by any means—graphic, electronic, or mechanical, including photocopying or information storage and retrieval systems—without written permission from the publisher.

The scanning, uploading, and distribution of this book or any part thereof via the Internet or via any other means without the permission of the publisher is illegal and punishable by law. Please purchase only authorized editions and do not participate in or encourage the electronic piracy of copyrighted materials.
"Schiffer," "Schiffer Publishing, Ltd. & Design," and the "Design of pen and inkwell" are registered trademarks of Schiffer Publishing, Ltd.

Type set in MetaPlusNormal/FagoNo/WarnockPro/Times New Roman/EANLinP36

ISBN: 978-0-7643-4591-3
Printed in China

Published by Schiffer Publishing, Ltd.
4880 Lower Valley Road
Atglen, PA 19310
Phone: (610) 593-1777; Fax: (610) 593-2002
E-mail: Info@schifferbooks.com

For our complete selection of fine books on this and related subjects, please visit our website at www.schifferbooks.com. You may also write for a free catalog.

This book may be purchased from the publisher.
Please try your bookstore first.

We are always looking for people to write books on new and related subjects. If you have an idea for a book, please contact us at proposals@schifferbooks.com.

Schiffer Publishing's titles are available at special discounts for bulk purchases for sales promotions or premiums. Special editions, including personalized covers, corporate imprints, and excerpts can be created in large quantities for special needs. For more information, contact the publisher.

EDITORIAL DIRECTION: María Fernanda Canal
EDITOR: Marta R. Hidalgo
AUTHOR OF CONTENT: Ángel Fernández
TEXT: Daniela Santos Quartino
ART DIRECTION: Mídori
GRAPHIC DESIGN AND MAKE UP: Pilar Cano
TRANSLATION: Luke Moreland
DIRECTION OF PRODUCTION: Rafael Marfil
PRODUCTION: Manel Sánchez

ORIGINALLY PUBLISHED AS:
Diseño de Estampados: de la idea al print final
© 2009 ParramonPaidotribo—World Rights
Published by Parramon Paidotribo, S.L., Badalona, Spain

OTHER SCHIFFER BOOKS BY THE AUTHOR:
Designing Fashion Accessories: Master Class in Professional Design, $45.00
ISBN: 978-0-7643-4215-8

OTHER SCHIFFER BOOKS ON RELATED SUBJECTS:
Emerging Fashion Designers, $39.99
ISBN: 978-0-7643-3600-3

Emerging Fashion Designers 3, $39.99
ISBN: 978-0-7643-4029-1

African Prints: A Design Book, $24.95
978-0-7643-0694-5

6 INTRODUCTION

8 DEVELOPMENT OF THE PROJECT: the creative process
    10 THE DESIGNER'S STUDIO: tools and working materials
    14 THE CLIENT
    18 RESEARCH AND DOCUMENTATION
    26 THE SKETCHBOOK: laboratory of ideas
    30 INSPIRATION: moodboards
    34 INTRODUCTION TO COLOR THEORY
    38 MOTIFS
    42 DEFINING THE IDEA
    46 DEVELOPMENT OF THE COLLECTION
    50 TRADITIONAL AND DIGITAL TECHNIQUES

58 FROM THE IDEA TO THE PRODUCT: the technical process
    60 PRESENTATION OF THE DESIGN
    64 POSITIONAL PRINTS AND *RAPPORT*
    72 TECHNIQUES OF USE

76 APPLYING THE DESIGNS TO FABRIC: the final result
    78 THE RAW MATERIAL
    96 DYES, VARNISHES, AND PIGMENTS
    98 FINAL PROCESSES OF PRINTING: screenprinting, devoré, digital printing, embroidery, roller printing, thermotransference, block printing, resist printing
    124 THE FINAL PRODUCT

130 STYLES AND MOTIFS: gallery
    132 BOTANICAL GARDEN
    Flowers, foliage, romanticism, pop inspiration
    140 GEOMETRY
    Lines and circles
    146 SPORT LIFE
    The sea, the mountains, the city, the countryside
    152 FAIRY TALES
    Stories and fables
    158 NOAH'S ARK
    Real and imaginary animals
    166 EXOTIC TRIPS
    Africa, Asia, South America
    172 LETTERS AND NUMBERS
    Ideas and messages
    178 ART
    From Baroque to Bauhaus and the Abstract
    186 NEW ROMANTIC
    Designs from the imagination

190 INDEX AND ACKNOWLEDGEMENTS

As a product of the art and creative genius of fashion designers, the collections that reach the public stage every season are valued according to two basic criteria: the pattern making and the raw materials, or textiles. A good knowledge of these two dimensions will provide the designer with the maximum freedom to represent his or her ideas and will contribute towards establishing the designer as a creator with a distinct identity. As the famous motto of the teacher Cristóbal Balenciaga goes, "the fashion designer must be an architect of the lines, a sculptor of the form, a painter of the color, a musician of the harmony, and a philosopher of the measurements." In this context, the designers work with a series of techniques and processes to create, give, sculpt, decorate, draw, and treat the textile. However, even though it seems obvious that the fabrics are part of the foundations of the clothes, the creation, development, and manipulation of the materials are aspects that generally remain hidden in the art of fashion. But it is true that, from fashion brands' casualwear collections up to the most exclusive creations that lead the catwalks of the high couture of Paris, printing is a basic part of the work of every designer. Because of this, a T-shirt with a basic pattern assumes a unique identity that can manage even to convert into a piece of cult fashion, thanks to the appearance of the graphic motifs that are applied on it. That's why printing is a process that requires skill and creativity to define the motifs, as well as some knowledge of the techniques and possibilities available to apply them on raw material.

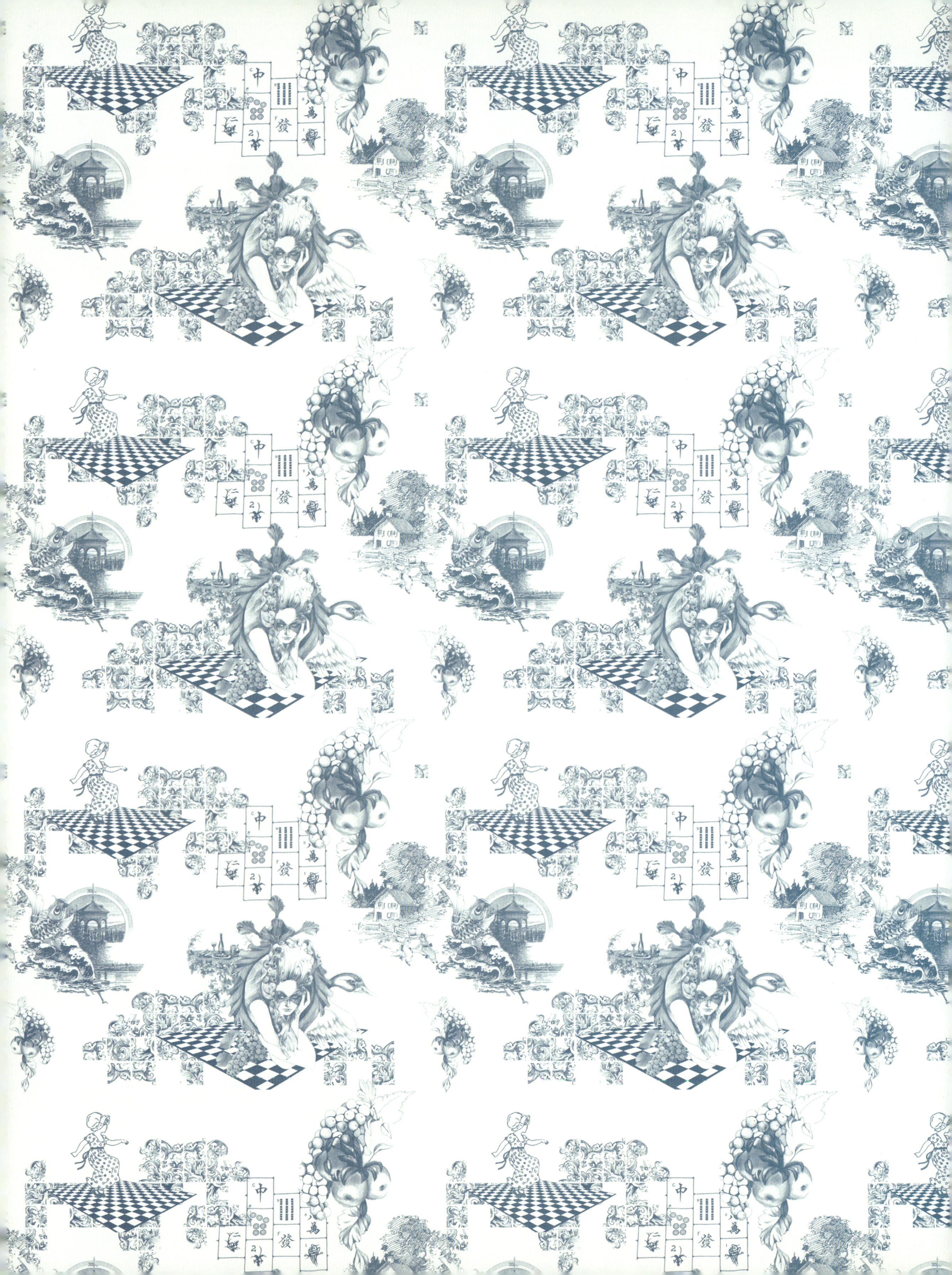

DEVELOPMENT OF THE PROJECT
the creative process

THE DESIGNER'S STUDIO
tools and working materials

The influence of the atmosphere is a key factor in the creative process. Because of that, the designer's workspace not only satisfies the need for organization and movement, but reflects their world as well. The studio is therefore a surprising area, full of magic, that invites inspiration.

A well-structured studio must always have good ventilation, good views, and a space for relaxation. As for the furniture, it is important to be equipped with desks of sufficient space, ergonomic chairs, and a library for organizing books, magazines, catalogs and movies.

Powerful digital equipment is another basic component. The computer will have to have a scanner and a printer with a great layout, and it is also convenient to have an integrated photocopying machine.

Generally, textile designers combine classic and digital techniques, which allow for a greater range of effects.

The great quantity of materials that one uses requires bookshelves to place the watercolors, inks, pencils, paintbrushes, gouache, and sprays, as well as an area for cleaning the tools.

Every company, or studio, has a different structure. Some companies depend on a textile design department and others use external design studies. The studio may be completed with a workshop where one can fabricate the screens of silk for screenprinting and test the fabrics, although this space is not an obligatory condition, since this part of the creative process can be carried out in external workshops especially set up for such purposes.

Normally, a studio of designers counts on several people directed by a creative director that presents them with work and is in charge of the follow-up. In the same way, every designer has a different form of organization, and it is possible to find teams in which everyone works individually on different projects.

1. The organization of tools is essential for the development of the job.

2-3. The studio of textile designers Lise Gulassa (California) and Cyrille Gulassa (Austria). From the company Sisters Gulassa.

the designer's studio 11

TOOLS AND WORKING MATERIALS

A deep knowledge of artistic materials and their creative possibilities grants great freedom in using the techniques available to represent ideas. If the designer gets used to a single technique, he or she will probably encounter obstacles when trying to satisfy the demands of different customers. That's why it is important that he or she has good equipment and materials.

GRAPHITE PENCILS
Graphite pencils are the basic tools used most often to define drawings. The pencil is formed by a mixture of pulverized natural graphite and clay that has been baked to a specific temperature. According to the hardness of the lead, a bigger or smaller proportion of graphite-clay is used. The more clay, the greater the hardness.

Hard lead pencils contain a narrower, dry lead of grayish tone. The softest have an oily lead that is fragile, dark, and thicker. The graphite pencil is the best way to draw monochrome figures with linear strokes that underline its profile.

MECHANICAL PENCILS
Mechanical pencils have a push button that allows the release of the lead, or graphite, to control the amount one uses. Their application is varied in the different phases of the design. The mechanical pencil can be used with a lead of 0.5 mm for sketching or to scribble ideas in a notebook, or with leads of 0.3 to 0.9 mm that, besides being useful for the first stages of the drawing, allow greater quality and precision in the details. There are an equal amount of varieties of lead hardness in mechanical pencils as there are in conventional pencils. They also offer the advantage of not having to be sharpened.

PASTELS AND CHARCOAL PENCIL
Pastels are composed of dry pigment pulverized and mixed with a combining agent. The resulting paste forms the bars, or leads, of a characteristic color. This tool is the nearest to pure color, as almost no intervention exists from elements foreign to the pigment. The charcoal pencil consists of powder mixed with a greasy agent that allows a thick and intense stroke.

COLORED PENCILS
Pencils with colored leads provide subtle lines as well as vivid strokes. They are very clean and they hardly need maintenance. Their handling does not differ too much from the conventional pencil. Only two aspects should be taken into account: the stroke cannot blur and its greasy consistency prevents a complete erasure with rubber. According to their material of manufacture, colored pencils are presented in several categories, including watercolor.

FELT-TIP PENS AND MARKERS
Felt-tip pens represent the most modern techniques of drawing and are especially used for illustration or publicity projects. The work process with felt-tip pens is similar to that of colored pencils, and they offer splendid results when they are used in combination. The felt-tip pen has a structure similar to the pen, as it contains its own ink. The tip of the felt-tip pen is usually made of a porous material, like felt.

INKS AND PAINTBRUSHES
Ink is a liquid substance with a high pigmentation power capable of providing a clear stain, with contrast and precision if it is thick, and sinuous, transparent, and delicate if its intensity is reduced with water. Chinese ink—one of the oldest varieties—is the thickest. The pigmented inks, for their part, contain other components, such as varnishes, to assure the adherence of the pigment to the surface and to prevent its elimination by the effects of mechanical abrasion. These materials are generally resins (in solvent inks) or composites (in water inks).

COLOR INKS AND WATERCOLORS
The watercolor technique is based on the effects of transparency, and allows the pigment to be diluted in water when it is settling on the white surface of the paper. This same principle guides work with color inks, also known among designers as aniline, or liquid, watercolors. In general, they are applied with round paint brushes.

GOUACHE AND ACRYLIC
Gouache and acrylic paints share many characteristics, even if their constitutions are very different. They are both water-soluble paints, although once the acrylic paint dries it is permanent and presents a glossy brightness. The gouache, on the other hand, is matt, provides better cover once dry, and dissolves with only one extra passing over with a wet paintbrush. Both paints work with paintbrushes, round as well as flat. In spite of the resemblance, both paints should never be mixed in the same job.

SUPPORTS FOR THE DRAWING: PAPER AND NOTEBOOKS
Paper is one of the most recurrent supports among fashion designers, although in the presentation of the projects this can be accompanied by samples of fabric and supporting textures that complement the design. The choice between the great existing variety of papers depends on the medium that will be used to draw. Grease-proof paper—fine, translucent, very soft, and waxy—is the most suitable. Because it is a transparent paper, it is used for transferring templates and images.

CAD EQUIPMENT *(computer aided design)*

Computer aided design (CAD) permits the insertion of images (original or scanned photographs) and manipulates them later with programs for drawing and a finishing touch. The possibilities are almost infinite. This method is faster and cleaner than the previous ones, but its application requires knowledge of the computer programs available for the design. The uses of these tools range from applications based on vectors and systems of drawing in two dimensions (2D) to pattern makers in three dimensions (3D). You can control the geometrical data (points, lines, arcs, etc.) that the programs use to interact with a graphic and variable interface.

1. Drawing of a pencil carried out manually and colored with inks. From the company Ailanto.

2. Composition carried out on a computer with images taken from books. It is printed on a grease-proof paper (tracing paper) in order to draw with graphite pencil.

3-4. Drawing notebook with flowers colored with watercolors, and box with Chinese paintbrushes of different thicknesses.

the designer's studio 13

THE CLIENT

When designers have their own textile companies, they do not have restrictions—except the market—regarding the public, to whom they want to direct their business, or to the type of designs that they can carry out. However, this situation characterizes not more than a small minority of companies. Generally, the client is the one who determines the direction that the designs will have to take, from the moment the client marks a target audience and a style. In these cases, it is the fashion or fabrics company that demands the work of the designer.

If the assignment comes from a fashion company, the designer will have the profile of their customer beforehand. Thus, the project will depend on the final purchaser of the garment: their age, sex, social status, purchasing power, and style (sporting, classic, luxury, etc.). The target audience is therefore usually a segment of the population selected according to these characteristics, and with a level of homogeneity. Much of the success of the design will depend on the extensive knowledge of this segment of the population.

The goal of the designer is to satisfy the wishes of the clients—but of course, always from his or her personal vision and style, which is, all in all, of the most precious value and the reason why the client has chosen this person to carry out the design of the clothes line.

1. The creations of Divinas Palabras were marketed to a young audience, informal and intellectual, who pays attention to the printed message on the garment.

2-3-4. The work of the textile designer Marcus James adapts to the requirements of different commercial companies. These designs and the final applications on the garment are assignments for the brands Yves Saint Laurent (2008 collection) and Camilla Staerk (Fall/Winter 2006 and Spring/Summer 2007 collections).

14 DEVELOPMENT OF THE PROJECT: the creative process

the client 15

Faithful to her style, the textile designer Hanna Werning has developed a concept line that has been applied to garments and accessories of the company House of Dagmar in different seasons.

16 DEVELOPMENT OF THE PROJECT: the creative process

The application of ribbons, fabrics, and embroideries has been chosen as the connecting thread of the designs that compose the first collection of Alta Costura in Paris, by the designer Josep Font.

RESEARCH AND DOCUMENTATION

Few creative endeavors require being as constantly aware of the latest trends as a fashion designer. Whether following the direction of trends or creating a totally divergent personal style, the designer must always be on alert, as if she were a "coolhunter," always compiling all the information presently available.

In their search for inspiration, the designers must investigate constantly. They must keep their eyes open to the channels of information in the fashion world (Internet, parades, fairs, books, museums, stores, trends of the market, etc.), assimilate subtle aesthetic changes, and observe the behaviors and tastes of the people.

So, as far as trends are concerned, the designer must scrutinize their immediate environment on-the-fly, in search of subjects or motifs to incorporate into their designs. However, it is also of extreme importance to be aware of new fabrics and printing techniques. In this sense, the Internet offers an almost infinite world of information. A good way of obtaining a great selection of interesting images is to get in touch with web sites specialized in fashion and trends, such as wgsn.com, instyle.com, stylesight.com, fashiontrendsetter.com, or trendunion.com, among others.

On the other hand, magazines, specialized fashion publications, and trade show catalogs help design and style professionals keep in contact with the big fashion designers of the world's main centers of creation: Paris, London, New York, Milan. If the designer has the opportunity to travel, he or she can attend design competitions, parades, fairs, and trade shows of fabrics and accessories. This is, essentially, one way of going directly to the sources of the fashion industry.

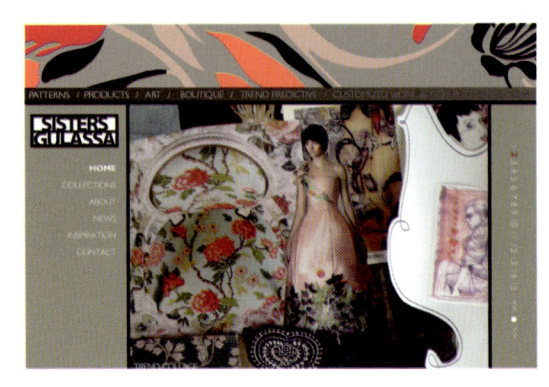

Websites that specialize in fashion are an indispensable reference for remaining up to date with the latest trends.

The personal library of the designer is an inexhaustible source of inspiration.

research and documentation 19

TRENDS

A trend is a pattern of behavior of the elements of a particular environment during a specific period of time. In less abstract terms, it refers to the things that are in fashion, or that are about to be in fashion. The act of capturing trends relies on the intuition of the designer, combined with the information that the environment offers. These themes set the guidelines by which the designer should work.

The creative textile designer always works one step ahead of street fashion. From the moment they invent their designs, a season goes by before the product arrives at the trade circuit. That's why it is vital that the designer knows in advance what so-called "street fashion" demands. Sometimes the designer is capable of predicting the trends, but the market may not yet be ready. In those cases it is better to save the ideas for the future, although there is always the possibility to present them in the most avant-garde sectors.

The specialized trade shows, which take place in the main centers of fashion production, are other sources of valuable information for the designer. This type of event allows one to know the trends at least a year in advance, establish contact with the sources of the fashion industry, and gather first-hand relevant innovations concerning anticipated charts and colors, types of fibers and fabrics, and new lines for the creation of garments for men, women, and children.

Another way of keeping up to date is to access reports from the numerous fashion professionals who travel around the world compiling data to publish in fashion magazines, or those compiled specifically for fashion companies. In this field there are departments that specialize in predicting the trends for the different areas of fashion and textiles. These entities offer the designers ideas on color, textures, motifs, silhouettes, and other aspects that will be trendy in forthcoming seasons. Some designers prefer to remain in the margin of trends and of all this information and work according to their personal tastes and intuition without letting the market influence them, perhaps thinking of a more exclusive public or with the intention of being the pioneer of a new style or trend.

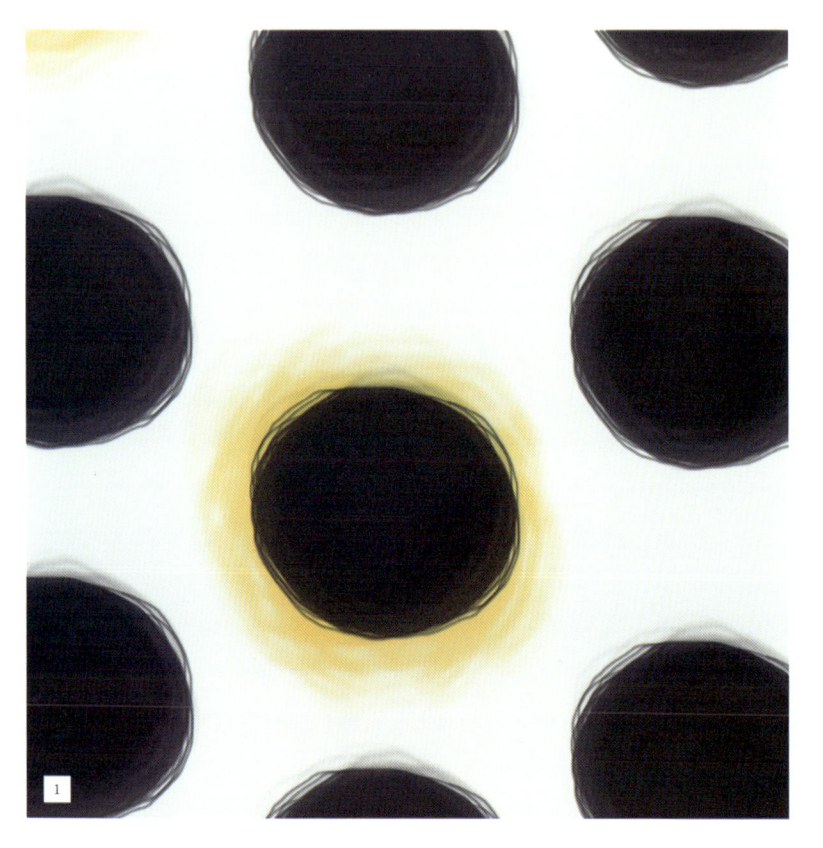

1. Polka dots are a motif that trends take up through the different seasons in versions according to each period (WGSN).

2. The digital treatment of the figures gives rise to multiple visual effects that the designer uses to generate variants on the same drawing (WGSN).

3. The traditional motif of the swan acquires a new dimension thanks to the use of digital techniques. From Marcus James for the company Camilla Staerk.

4. Designs that are shown on the catwalk influence the brands of "high street" to create trends that arrive to the general consumer. From Marcus James for the company Camilla Staerk.

research and documentation

1. Exhibitions of international interest can be influential in fashion, as it has happened on repeated occasions with the Japanese artist Utamaro, whose drawings are printed on this handkerchief of silk.

2. The figures inspired by Japanese culture always have been in the line of sight of trends because of the appeal of their delicate forms and the combination of colors.

3. Detail of Japanese kimono in silk painted by hand.

4. Illustration carried out with the technique of templates and spray, often used on street art. From the company Ailanto.

22 DEVELOPMENT OF THE PROJECT: the creative process

Details of prints on silk for wedding kimonos. The floral motifs and the geometry are recurrent inspirations for Japanese creators.

research and documentation **23**

SHOWS

Textile shows present twice a year the latest trends and innovations in woven and printed materials, before the following seasons: Spring/Summer and Fall/Winter. These exhibitions are, at the same time, a platform for designers and an area in which the creative can show their works and sell the textile manufacturers and designers their works in fashion. One of the most important shows of the sector is celebrated in Paris and is called Première Vision (www.premierevision.fr). Textile manufacturers and designers form around the world are brought together in the French capital to buy and to sell their product or to discover first-hand the novelties of the sector.

Alongside this exhibition, other meetings take place, such as Expofil, dedicated to fibers and spinning, Le Cuir à Paris, dedicated to skin and leather, and Indigo, specializing in textile design, printing, embroideries, and vintage material. As important as that of Paris is the show that is celebrated in Florence, Pitti Filati, subsidiary of the exhibitions of Pitti Immagine, to which experts of the entire world go (www.pittimmagine.com).

Other important textile shows celebrated every year in different cities of the world are:

PREMIÈRE VISION NEW YORK: preview of trends in fabrics. New York (United States). www.premierevision-newyork.com

PREMIÈRE VISION MOSCOU: preview of trends in fabrics. Moscow (Russia). www.premierevision.ru

TEXWORLD: latest trends in fabrics. Paris (France); New York (United States); Mumbai (India).
www.textworld.messefrankfurt.com

SALÓN TEXTIL INTERNACIONAL DE BARCELONA: presentation of the principal collections of fabrics. Barcelona (Spain). www.stib.net

IDEABIELLA: fabrics for men's and women's fashion. Milan (Italy). www.ideabiella.it

IDEACOMO: fabrics for feminine fashion. Milan (Italy). www.ideacomo.com

MODA IN: vanguard materials for the fashion market. Milan (Italy). www.fieramodain.it

PRATO EXPO: innovative fabrics for casual fashion for men and women. Milan (Italy). www.pratoexpo.com

SHIRT AVENUE: fabrics for shirt making. Milan (Italy). www.shirt-avenue.com

MUNICH FABRIC START: international fabrics fair. Munich (Alemania). www.munichfabricstart.com

TECHTEXTIL: international monograph fair. Atlanta and Las Vegas (United States); Frankfurt (Germany); Shanghai (China); Mumbai (India); Moscow (Russia).

INTERTEXTILE: fabrics for dress making and furniture. Beijing and Shanghai (China). www.messefrankfurt.com.hk

YARN ESPO: international fibers and yarns show. Shanghai (China). www.messefrankfurt.com.hk

PITTIFILATI: knitted fabrics. Florence (Italy). www.pittimmagine.com

A similar motif, like the arabesques, is presented through a large number of variants, thanks to the application of different drawing and printing techniques. These designs of the company Lissa were shown in the show Première Vision Paris, Winter 2008.

research and documentation 25

SKETCHBOOK laboratory of ideas

Sketchbooks, or notebooks, are the first step in the process of creating a print. In them ideas are represented, creating something similar to a visual journal in which some concepts are highlighted that will be accepted or discarded with time. Sketchbooks are a space for testing and where ideas materialize in drawings. They are a personal file in which images are stored that come to the designer from numerous sources: museums, magazines, parades, movies, books, or the street.

The sketchbook includes the necessary conceptual material to complete a printing idea. This includes design, color, and three-dimensional pieces. Any object serves well if it provides something new and interesting: from a newspaper clipping to a sample of fabric, the leaf of a tree, and even photographs of characters, trips, or the environment. This ensemble alone produces great visual pieces coherently enough that it becomes the best tool available for the designer to view her creations before making them public.

It has to be taken into account that at first, the drawings, notes, and designs developed in a notebook do not have a public character. Because of this, they provide an opportunity to work without inhibitions or outside judgments, which is suitable for creating the boldest designs. A sketchbook contains very personal information about the designer. This is its principal value, for this kind of information can generate original ideas, and as a rule, it must not be revealed prematurely.

There are several ways of sketching projects, but the most common is through the pencil, as drawing is an important part of the process of design. In these drawings, the stroke must be agile, scribbled, synthetic, and imprecise.

Generally, it is not conceived as a perfect illustration, but as a sketch that only the author himself can endow with meaning.

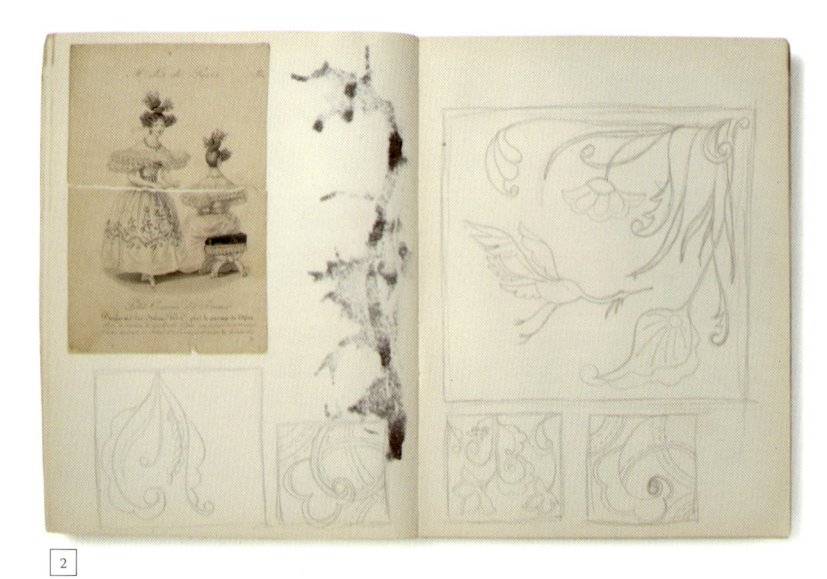

26 DEVELOPMENT OF THE PROJECT: the creative process

THE DRAWING

The drawings in the sketchbook lack refinement because their principal mission is to roughly reflect an idea. The goal of these sketches is to draw a line, to comprise in an abbreviated form indications of style or color.

It is for this reason that most of these drawings are executed with great speed, which in turn gives greater spontaneity and freshness to the stroke. The drawings, although sketched, must be easily legible or interpretable for the author, for their purpose is to clarify ideas and concepts.

For many designers, the sketchbook has a completely digital function, not only because their ideas and information come from the computer—either through the Internet or from images that they collect with a digital camera—but also because they carry out the drawings using computer programs.

Although it is true that computers make available an enormous library for inspiration, as well as infinite possibilities of effects that would make pencil, paper, and cutouts unnecessary, their excitement as a novelty has passed. At present, the trend is to go back to the classic techniques, as far as drawing is concerned.

To remember and to process better what she has observed, the designer refers to notes written on the margin of every drawing. This way, one can add information about the colors, the textures, and the tonal values. These annotations are necessary for preliminary presentations to the customer or to the tailor. Thus, in these cases, the sketches are accompanied by appendixes with notes that reveal important details, as well as subjective impressions, such as dates, localities, indications of color, points for the embroidery, or types of fabric.

1-2-3-4. The sketchbook is a visual journal in which the first concepts of a print are recorded, accompanied by notes with specifications on textures and the colors.

5. Sketches are designed to clarifying ideas and concepts that afterwards will be represented in the fabric.

the sketchbook 27

Research on variations of motifs of the same color in drawings carried out with aniline and bleach, from the notebook of Javier Nanclares.

28 DEVELOPMENT OF THE PROJECT: the creative process

The same motif: (1) drawn by hand on paper, (2) sketched digitally, and (3) as prototype on a garment.

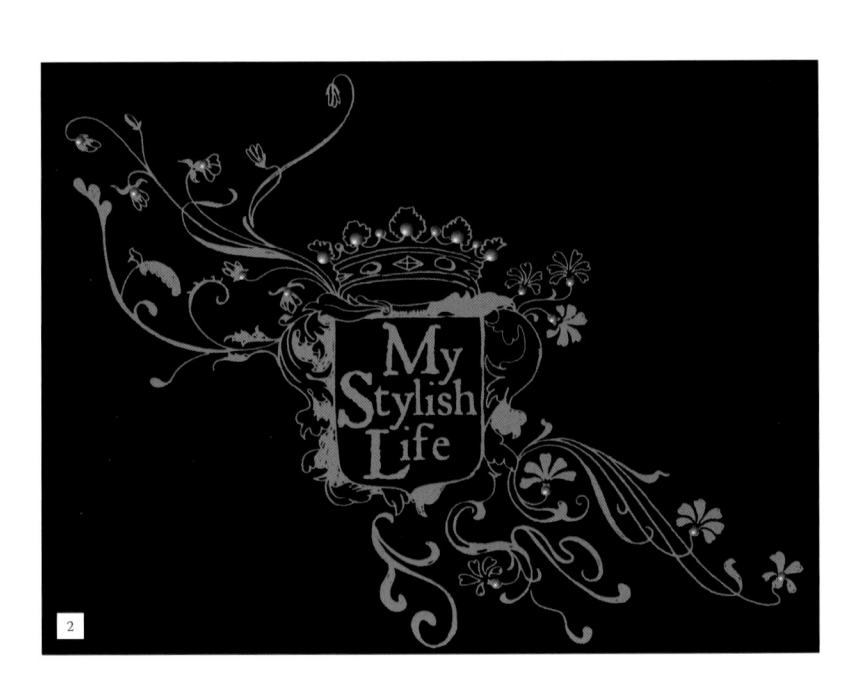

the notebook **29**

INSPIRATION moodboards

Inspiration is combined with constant research, which involves the designer keeping his eyes open to the channels of information in the fashion world in order to assimilate the subtle aesthetic changes it produces. It could be said that a designer is like a radar that perceives the variations of the period and the concerns of the immediate environment, and incorporates them into his designs.

The process of compiling materials and images is a key step in the creation of motifs. For this, the designer uses a moodboard that accompanies and complements the sketchbook and brings together evocative images on the chosen subject. As its objective this trend panel acts as a source of inspiration as well as an instrument to generate and connect ideas.

This panel is a composition, carried out in paper or in digital format, in which the visual lines that have inspired the creation of a motif for its future printing are included. It is a collection of images extracted from magazines, books, the Internet, and photographs that, as a whole, give insight into the style one wants to reach.

This tablet of information, on which photographs of gadgets, garments, cutouts of fabrics, charts of color, and daily objects are accumulated and have been cut and put carefully in order, enable the grouping together of different ideas in one double-page spread. Once sufficient images have been compiled it is possible to start developing new designs. With time, these boards of information based on collages can turn into a useful file to go to in order to extract or recover ideas.

COLORING

In order to define coloring, the most universal language is that of Pantone (the company responsible for creating physical color charts for professionals). The Pantone colors that are used in the fashion world are those of TC finish (Pantone Textile Colors). When the designer delivers the original drawing to the workshop, the company producing the fabric will be in charge of finding the most accurate colors based on the Pantone color reference number or real samples.

Moodboard of images for inspiration created on a photobase. Original collage by Javier Nanclares.

Like a patchwork of ideas, the moodboard reveals sources for the designer. Collage of fabrics of wild silk accompanied with photographs of *Vogue Italia* as referents of style.

inspiration **31**

Moodboard for World Global Style Network (WGSN) coloring.

Color chart for the winter season of 2008-2009 of a commercial company.

Fabric color charts constitute a more exact approach as textures can cause tonal variations.

32 DEVELOPMENT OF THE PROJECT: the creative process

Prints where variations of color and drawing are shown for the same theme: optical motifs from a retro inspiration. From Laura Fernández for the company Simorra. Winter Collection 2008-2009.

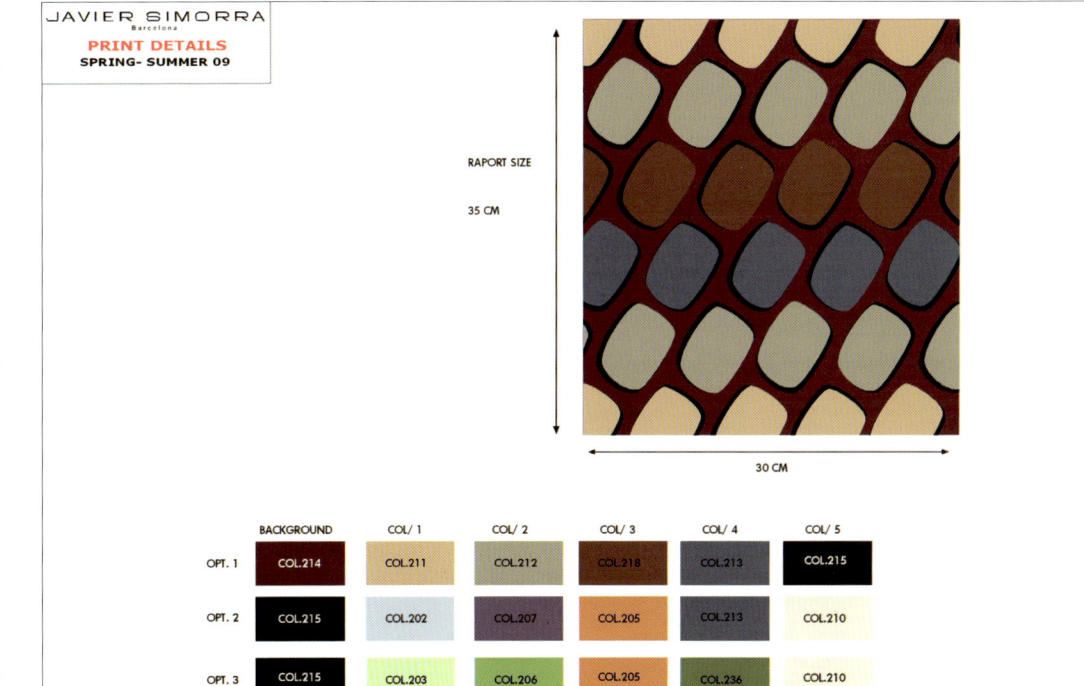

Technical data with color references.

Polka dots of different sizes. From Laura Fernández for the company Simorra. Winter Collection 2008-2009.

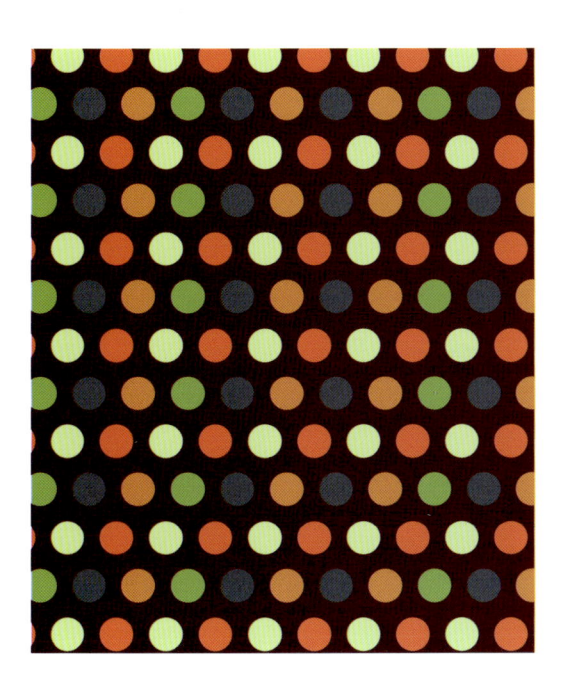

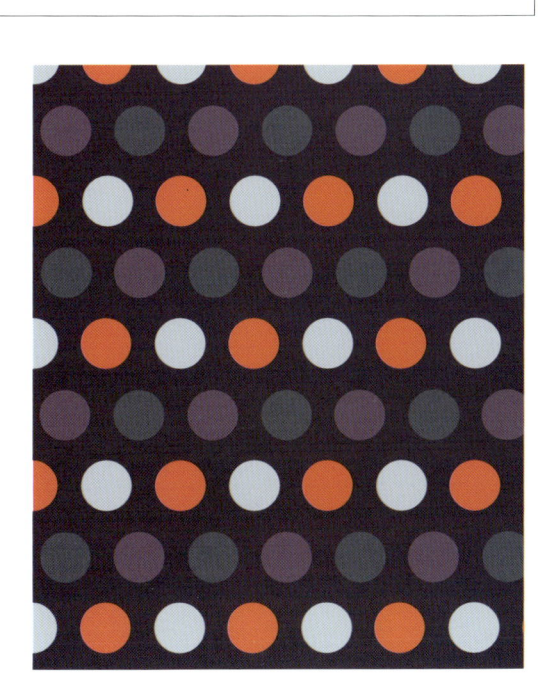

JAVIER SIMORRA
Barcelona
PRINT DETAILS
SPRING- SUMMER 09

RAPORT SIZE

35 CM

30 CM

	BACKGROUND	COL/ 1	COL/ 2	COL/ 3	COL/ 4	COL/ 5
OPT. 1	COL.214	COL.211	COL.212	COL.218	COL.213	COL.215
OPT. 2	COL.215	COL.202	COL.207	COL.205	COL.213	COL.210
OPT. 3	COL.215	COL.203	COL.206	COL.205	COL.236	COL.210

the notebook 33

INTRODUCTION TO COLOR THEORY

Colors are ordered in a graphic representation called a chromatic circle, which follows the guidelines of the breakdown of visible light in the solar spectrum. This classification comes from the interaction of three primary colors (magenta, yellow, and blue cyan) that can not be obtained by combining other colors. This means that they are totally autonomous and they do not resemble any other tone. The mixture of the primaries creates another three new colors (red, green, and violet) that are known as secondaries.

The chromatic circle is a very useful tool for viewing with clarity how colors interact among themselves and with their complementaries (those that occupy the opposed side of the circle). So, for example: yellow is the complementary color of violet, and therefore, both will still stand out more when one applies them together in a design.

When designs are made with a computer, it is important to make sure that the colors seen on the monitor are exactly the same as those that appear afterwards in the design applied to the garment. There are different methods for this, but, undoubtedly, the best way is to use hardware specific for that purpose.

RANGES OF COLOR

Mixing different proportions of primary and secondary colors creates new tones. Grouped together by chromatic resemblance, they form what are known as ranges. The warm palette is composed of colors that result from the mixture of yellow, red, ochre, and their derived tones: browns, orange, etc. Cold palettes are the result of mixing blues, violets, and greens. They can become lighter with white dyes and darker with greys and blues. The palette of achromatic colors is formed by the mixture of warm and cold colors. It has greyish tones and is presented as a range with very sober colors. The range of pastel colors, in turn, includes the tones in which the white color predominates.

HARMONY AND CONTRAST

Mastering contrast and harmony is a basic skill for the design of prints given the prominence that color has. The effect of contrasting colors prevents boredom and breaks the dullness of a collection. On the contrary, harmonic combinations involve similarity more than difference, thanks to the choice of colors that do not clash. The most effective way of assuring a harmonic combination is to rely on the analogous chromatic scheme—that is, to follow the order of the adjacent colors of a chromatic wheel. Using analogous colors may involve three or four adjacent shades with different degrees of brightness. In addition, it is very effective to create forms with contrasting colors that are warm and cold, light and dark, complementary, saturated, and achromatic.

In this regard, it is useful to take into account that when designing a subtle and slightly contrasted print, the contrast among the colors should be exaggerated slightly, to prevent losing small nuances.

Chromatic circle composed of twelve colors arranged according to the segment of the light.

34 DEVELOPMENT OF THE PROJECT: the creative process

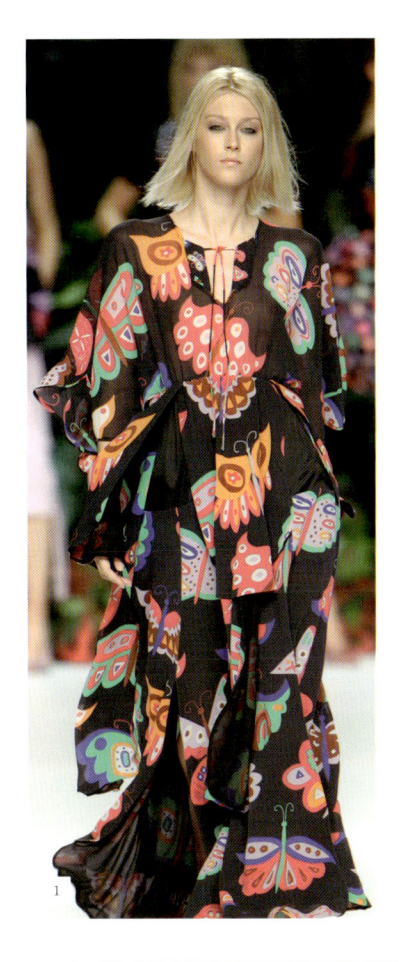

1-2-3. Colors and drawings have a principle role in the configuration of each of these garments that belong to different seasons. From the company Ailanto.

4. Final drawing with flowers of naive inspiration and preparation of colors to be printed on white or on any other color base. From the company La Casita de Wendy.

381U	381U
319U	319U
2582U	2582U
129U	129U
189U	189U
black	white

color 35

36 DEVELOPMENT OF THE PROJECT: the creative process

1. This vintage illustration painted by hand on silk is used as a guide for the creation of the color chart that will dominate in a collection.

2-3. Pop inspiration in floral motifs demonstrating variations of color on fabric and drawing the main motifs by hand on transparent paper. From Laura Fernández for the company Giulio.

4-5. Camouflage prints with different tonal variations. The warm colors are combined through harmony, and the cold colors through contrast. From Laura Fernández for Giulio.

color **37**

MOTIFS

A motif is the graphic interpretation of a concept applied in an isolated part of the fabric or in an organized composition. When the motif has been conceived for repetition, it can be duplicated until it occupies all the fabric. The motifs can be as varied as the designer's imagination. Anything that has form can be drawn in very different styles, from abstraction to precise detail.

Floral motifs are one of the most frequent resources in fashion printing, equal to geometrical motifs and ornaments. The combination of forms with variations of color creates results of an infinite variety. These results rise up from the imagination of the creator and are realized with the use of printing techniques.

EFFECTS

Textile drawings can modify the perception of the figure, conceal anatomical reliefs, and provide a dynamic perception of the piece. Thus, for example, skirts or dresses printed with horizontal, diagonal, or vertical stripes modify the perception of the silhouette of the body, making a person seem wider, thinner, taller, or shorter. On the other hand, the application of a motif in specific areas distracts attention from the rest of the garment. This is a resource that the designer will have to take into account at the time of promoting or disguising certain aspects of the figure.

1. White and black drawing for positional print in T-shirt. From Laura Fernández.

2-3. White and black motifs with vintage effects for collection of young masculine garments.

4-5. Designs with optical effects composed of the outline of concentric circles and waved lines.

the motifs **39**

1-2. The same line acquires a different depth and emphasis according to the drawing that is applied over it. In the composition, which is formed by an illustration and a photograph, the lines seem more tenuous than in the orchid print. By Rafa Mollar.

3. Floral design in soft colors for application on fabric (WGSN).

40 DEVELOPMENT OF THE PROJECT: the creative process

the motifs 41

DEFINING THE IDEA

Before a collection becomes part of the culture, the designers work hard to give form to a concept that grants value to their creation. Designers put their knowledge, intuition, sensitivity, and information collected from multiple sources into practice until they arrive at the idea they want to convey.

Ideas are of even greater importance today, since competing for price is not an option anymore, and quality and design are the most valuable attributes of a collection. Fashion companies have to create a brand and a style that distinguishes them, and this is obtained through the designer's ideas. That's why, before starting to design a collection, it is necessary to develop a line from a unique source of inspiration. The line should have a design and a range of colors and textures that give it coherence and relate it to a story or concept.

It is helpful to start the process by writing down all the ideas that come to you, taking into account the creative possibilities, originality, and versatility that each theme allows for, and especially the profile of the final customer: the public, for whom the garment is destined. Drawings are good for establishing the essence of the concept. Further along, once the sketches start to reinforce an image, one can proceed to add colors and samples of fabrics that complete the representation.

1-2. Both of these prints have been made from an original idea: an abstraction based on decorations from animals and a figurative drawing with scenes of celebrations in high society. From the company Basso & Brooke.

3-4-5-6. Famous flower and animal prints of Hanna Werning transferred to backpacks for the company Eastpak, collection 2005.

42 DEVELOPMENT OF THE PROJECT: the creative process

Name: GRASSHOPPER LUCK

Eastpak
January 2004

Hanna Werning
Spring Street Studio
Stockholm / London
+46 (0)70 236 57 25
www.byhanna.com
hello@byhanna.com

FISHPOND FLUSH

Eastpak
14 February 2005

Hanna Werning
Spring Street Studio
Stockholm / London
+46 (0)70 236 57 25
www.byhanna.com
hello@byhanna.com

Name: OCEAN STAR

Eastpak
3 January 2004

Hanna Werning
Spring Street Studio
Stockholm / London
+46 (0)70 236 57 25
www.byhanna.com
hello@byhanna.com

defining the idea 43

Sometimes the textile designer's work is so transcendent that some customers make it part of their own personal style. The renowned cartoonist Hanna Werning has developed prints for the House of Dagmar and Anna Sui, among other feminine fashion.

define the idea **45**

DEVELOPMENT OF THE COLLECTION

Once the type of business or client for whom the designer will work is specified, the style is defined, and the process of research is completed, she finally has a story to tell. The final idea is translated into a collection in which the designer should give an indication as to the source of inspiration, the theme of the project, and its intentions. The necessary ingredients for developing a collection are creativity, boldness, a critical attitude, curiosity, a capacity for synthesis, flexibility, an innovative spirit, artistic sensitivity and, of course, technical and material knowledge.

It is necessary to display a wide range of ideas that work not only individually, but also show coherence with the collection. A systematic approach to such important factors as style, color, use of similar prints, and production contributes towards this coherence.

The collection requires keeping two visions in mind: one global, which establishes a link with the collection, and one individual. Just as each piece in a collection tells a story, each print should contain within it a unique world that speaks for itself.

In a collection there are usually "families," or subdivisions of the central theme, that form so as to obtain a repertoire with different offerings within the same theme. Variations may keep the motif as the unifying link and provide different groupings based on the colors.

One can also display the same drawing style, with changes, in a defined group of tones. Whenever you do this, it is very important to limit the options so that the idea is reinforced rather than lost in the infinite variables of the design.

1. The colors and the lines in the drawings of the dress reflect the global concept of the collection of the designer Miriam Ocáriz.

2. Dress and jacket of Miriam Ocáriz, collection Summer 2007.

3. Print of Ocáriz used in the collection Spring-Summer 2007. Once again, the color and the hand-drawn lines are made visible: signs that characterize the collections of this creator.

development of the collection 47

tul plumeti
CAN-CAN +
VESTIDO ESTAMPADO

48 DEVELOPMENT OF THE PROJECT: the creative process

1-2-3. View of the evolution of a design carried out in screenprinting (see page 103), from the sketch to the garment, and finally, the catwalk. Coherence is the key. From the company Miriam Ocáriz.

development of the collection 49

TRADITIONAL AND DIGITAL TECHNIQUES

On very few occasions we will find a designer who defines himself or herself with only one working technique. The more skills they master, the more likely they are to obtain a result that resembles their original idea. The successful communication of the concept that resides in every collection depends on the designer's comprehension of the advantages and limitations of different techniques.

Techniques can be classified as traditional or digital. The first set involves a form of craftsmanship: inks, watercolors, gouaches, and acrylic, which involve using paintbrushes or sponges. This category also includes what are called "dry techniques," like pencils and pastels, as well as oil paints (oils and oil pastels).

You will also find under traditional techniques the collage, which leads to innovative results through cutouts of photographs, paintings, and textures. Finally, another frequently used technique in printing is the stencil, which involves applying color with spray or sponge on templates.

Digital techniques rely on the use of a computer, which processes images and manipulates them through specific programs. With these, the representations may have a crafted or totally digital origin. If we choose the first option, the drawing is carried out through traditional techniques and is scanned afterwards to be able to convert it into a digital file and transform it with programs, such as Adobe Photoshop®, with a finishing touch of images. This last step provides variations in colors and sizes. With these programs it is also possible to put together digital collages by introducing images from different sources. The second option groups together drawings that are made directly on the computer with special programs made for these purposes, such as Adobe Illustrator®.

Today, almost all designers combine traditional and digital techniques. The starting point of their work is usually a scanned image or photographs that they manipulate digitally until they obtain the desired final result.

Different compositions from mixture of traditional techniques.

1. Sample that combines the mixture of traditional techniques: gouache, stencil, and collage. From the company Sisters Gulassa.

2. Collage obtained from the cutout of different superimposed fabrics. From the company Sisters Gulassa.

3. Print-on illustrations with watercolor technique. From the company Sisters Gulassa.

4. Floral-inspired motifs printed with gouache technique. From the company Sisters Gulassa

traditional and digital techniques 51

52 DEVELOPMENT OF THE PROJECT: the creative process

Different compositions from the mixture of digital and traditional techniques.

1. Floral composition with the use of different tones treated digitally. Design of Sisters Gulassa.

2. Different samples of screenprinting on paper from the company Sisters Gulassa.

3. Different examples in which the combination of traditional and digital techniques results in very attractive effects.

traditional and digital techniques 53

54 DEVELOPMENT OF THE PROJECT: the creative process

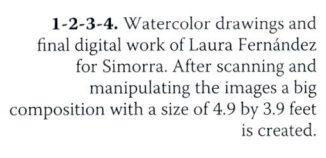

1-2-3-4. Watercolor drawings and final digital work of Laura Fernández for Simorra. After scanning and manipulating the images a big composition with a size of 4.9 by 3.9 feet is created.

5-6. Drawing of floral border with bird. After drawing the sketch the outline was drawn by hand with graphite pencil and afterwards, on a transparent paper, the chromatic characteristics were defined with colored pencils. Both drawings were scanned to create a document with two layers: one for the line and another for the color. The same motif was sent to India and was embroidered by hand in manila style on silk satin.

traditional and digital techniques

THE COLLAGE

For a designer to represent his or her creations in the best way possible, he or she must explore all the techniques at their disposal, and the collage acts as a good resource for stimulating their creativity. This practice involves assembling different elements in one unified whole. Throughout its development, it makes every combination of technique and style possible. This includes cutouts of images, threads, and fabrics stuck on a paper, or combinations of photographs and drawings in a digital document.

This technique is extremely useful for first defining the concept. In fact, it's like a brainstorming session with materials, which allows the designer to view combinations of textures, colors, and motifs before actually beginning. These representative possibilities may also function as a very good resource for submitting proposals to the customer.

1-2. Miscellaneous techniques and materials in collages from Miriam Ocáriz.

3-4-5-6. Drawing and prototypes of embroideries with collage of fabrics, applications, and varied stitches. By María José Lleonar for Simorra.

7-8. Photographic collage with kaleidoscope effect from the company La Casita de Wendy.

traditional and digital techniques **57**

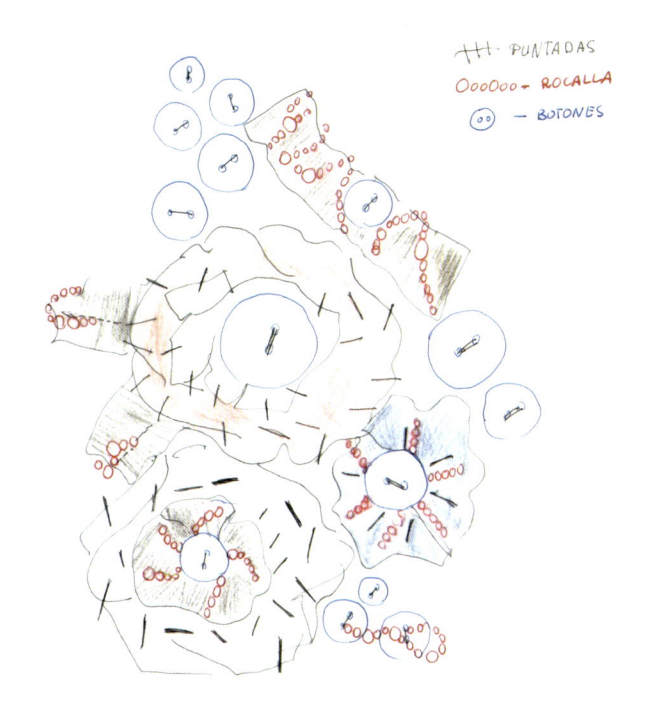

FROM THE IDEA TO THE PRODUCT
the technical process

PRESENTATION OF THE DESIGN

Presenting creative work to the production company requires the designer to use a language intelligible to all parties that also facilitates the translation of her ideas into the finished product. The first step of the supplier, before arriving at the production stage, consists of providing samples or prototypes of a garment or samples of cut fabric, following the guidelines marked by the designer. The supplier's samples will then undergo a series of adjustments for finishing touches, such as color and intensity, until arriving at the final result. Thus is set in motion the mechanisms that prepare the design for submission to industrial production: separating the color into layers, creating the crosshatching when it is necessary, and the rapport if one wants to repeat a drawing in a print. On other occasions, the designer himself is the one who prepares a digital document and a technical sheet in which all the necessary technical aspects for the production are detailed.

The designer, therefore, must know the techniques of the company the product is going to; that is, the different processes of printing that the company offers.

Likewise, it is also very important that one stays updated on the array of possibilities of handling fabrics that facilitate designs, such as dyes and materials that are used in different processes, since all these factors produce very different tactile and visual effects. In addition to personal creation, designers can go to special events and locations like international textile fairs or professional design studios and look for fabrics for their fashion collections. When all is said and done, you can buy original, handmade designs painted on fabric or paper, or embroidered, dyed, or digitally constructed designs, each already prepared for delivery to production. Sometimes you may only sell only the idea, and then you are in charge of the performing necessary technical preparations for the subsequent industrial process.

Finally, an alternative option involves purchasing the fabric already finished by a company that is in charge of the creative and technical process and offers the already finished product for creating the garments.

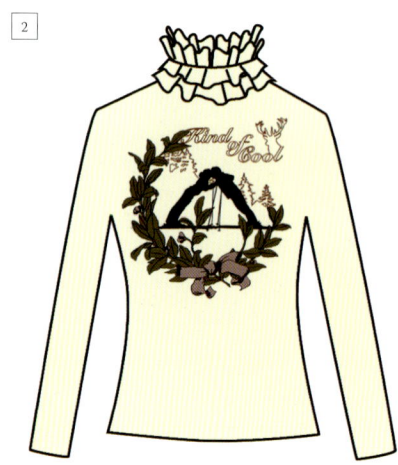

1. Detail of the printing motif and its location in the final garment in the presentation to the customer. By Laura Fernández.

2. General view of the garment with the final print.

3-4-5. Technical drawings separated by layers of color to print with screenprinting. The separation of color layers prepares the design technically so that it can be taken to industrial production.

6. Drawing of layers of color for embroidery.

60 FROM THE IDEA TO THE PRODUCT: the technical process

PRINT 2 brown

PRINT 1 BLACK

PRINT 3 pink

EMBROIDERY

presentation of the design 61

[1]

SEASON: SUMMER 2007 REF: XT-9 POSITIONAL DIAGRAM FOR EMBROIDERED DESIGN

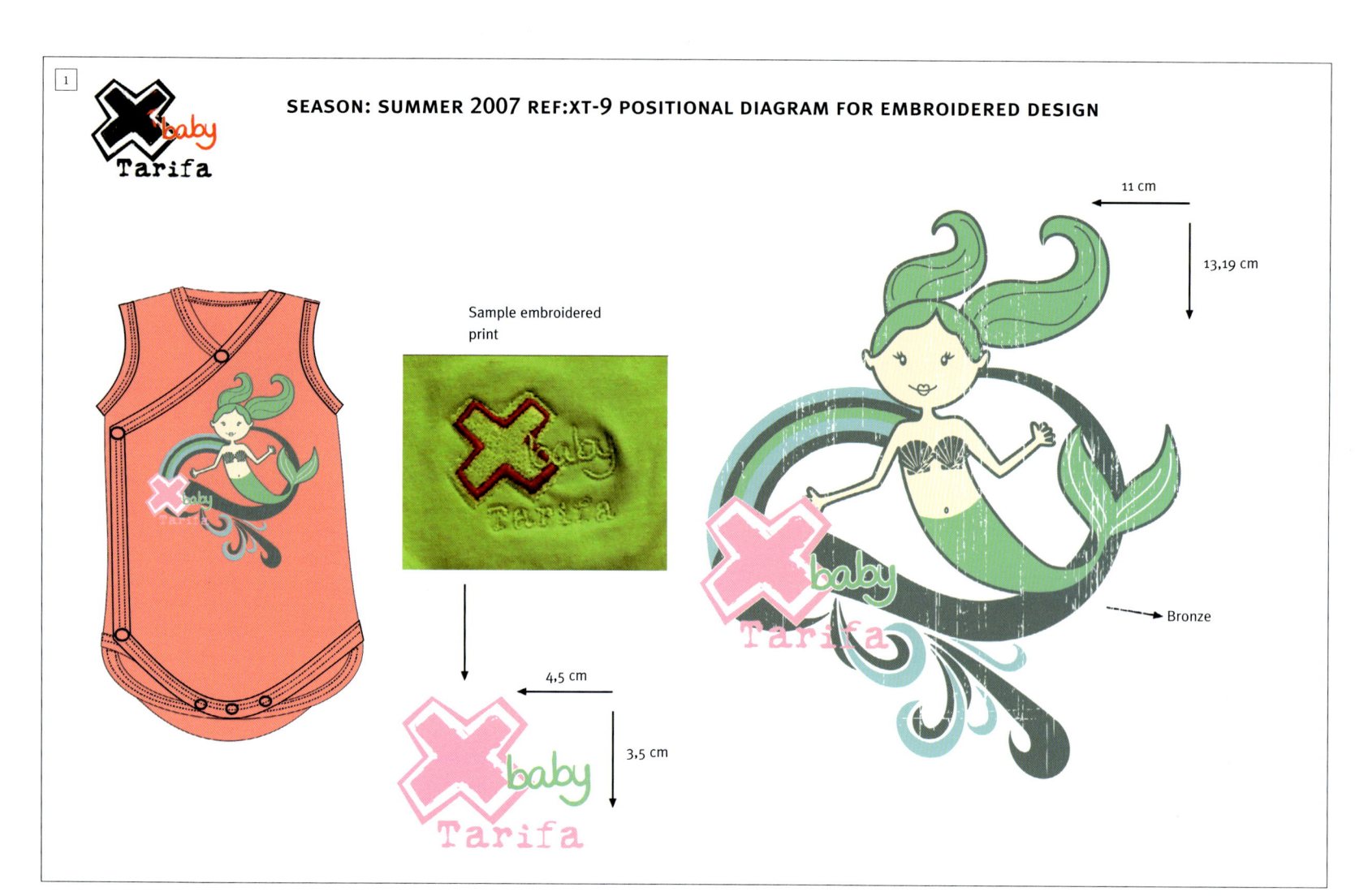

Sample embroidered print

11 cm

13,19 cm

4,5 cm

3,5 cm

Bronze

SEASON: SUMMER 2007 REF: XT-11 PRINT AND APPLIQUE

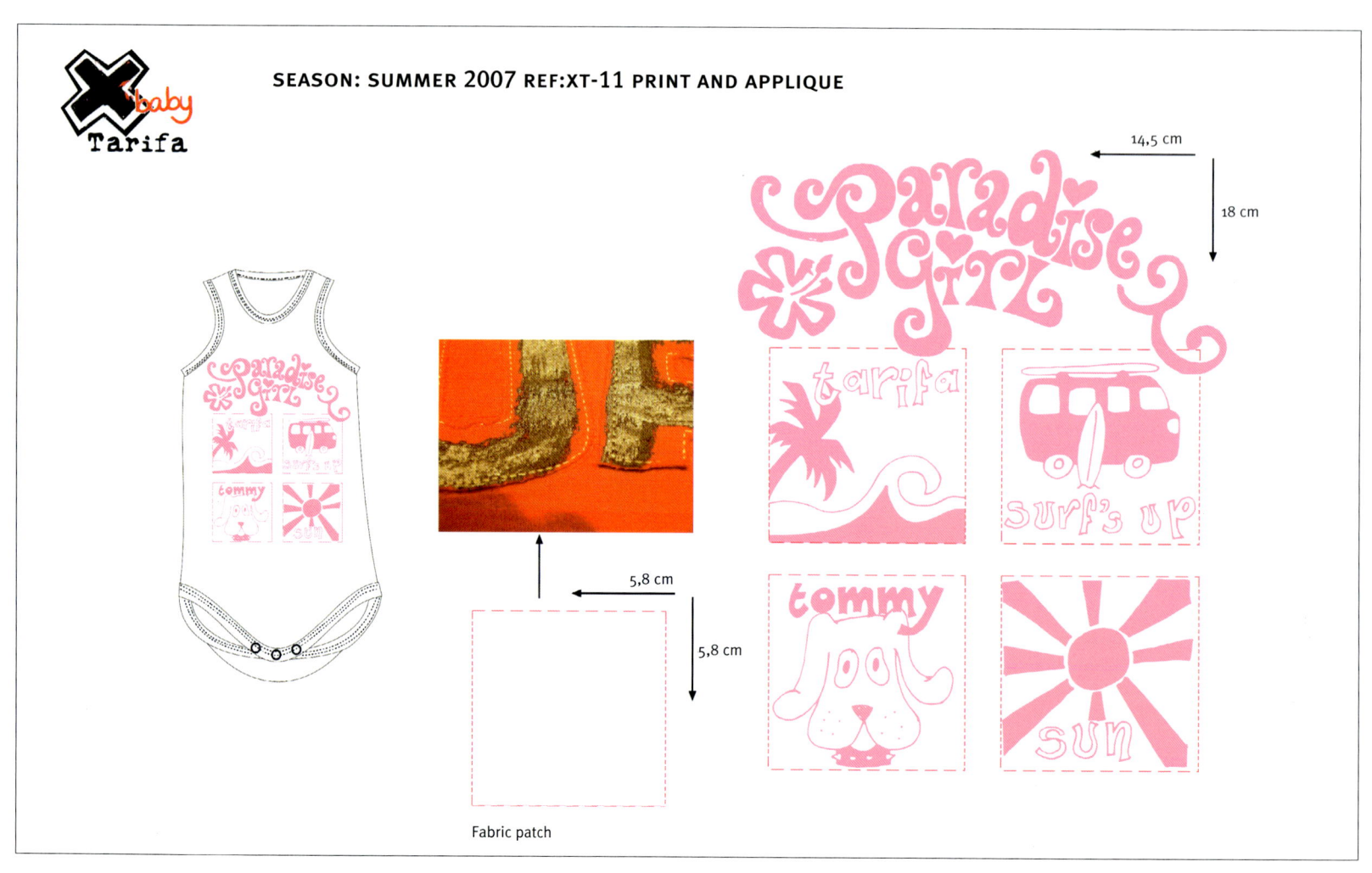

14,5 cm

18 cm

5,8 cm

5,8 cm

Fabric patch

62 FROM THE IDEA TO THE PRODUCT: the technical process

[2]

[3]

1. Technical sheets include references to the position of the print and the form of application. By Laura Fernández for Xbaby. Collection Spring-Summer 2007.

2-3-4-5. The designer Ligia Unanue creates unique prototypes of garments made of pieces sewn, painted, and decorated manually, which she uses to introduce lines to different commercial companies that specialize in clothing for babies.

[4]

[5]

presentation of the design **63**

POSITIONAL PRINTING AND RAPPORT

The application of illustrations is carried out in two ways: situating the image in a sector specific to the garment on a background of full color, or making the image take up the whole of the piece through the repetition of the original design.

The first method is known as positional printing and is carried out on the already cut or ready-made garment. This procedure requires that the designer specify the exact position of the print in the technical sheet, with precise coordinates. This type of print can be applied through screenprinting, hot stamping, or transfer, and embroideries. Screenprinting requires the preparation of different layers of color that will be printed on the shablón, or mold, whereas the transfer cuts back the drawing on a vinyl that afterwards is applied on the garment through heat.

Today, these types of designs are very common in the fashion world, and there are many companies that create drawings for decorating their garments. In the past, this type of printing was only frequent in the badges or logos of some garments and in music or souvenir T-shirts. Continuous prints, or rapport, are generally produced in a rotating system, in which a cylinder with the fabric engraving spins the garment around and keeps providing different layers of colors.

Another way of creating continuous prints is using flat screens in which the top of the drawings are fitted with the lower part to create continuity. If you desire this effect, you must take into account the width of the fabric and of the illustration so that it fits perfectly on the fabric. Some computer programs, which allow a wide range of design manipulations, are specially designed for this purpose.

1. Technical sheet for T-shirt with positional print. Design of Ximena Topolansky for the company Strong Enough.

2. Technical sheet for T-shirt with rapport. Design of Ximena Topolansky for the company Strong Enough.

3-4-5. Vector drawing based on a scanned photo of a vintage print. The resulting lines have been filled in with color to define the main motif. The rapport rises up from repeating the same motif in all directions. From the company Giulio.

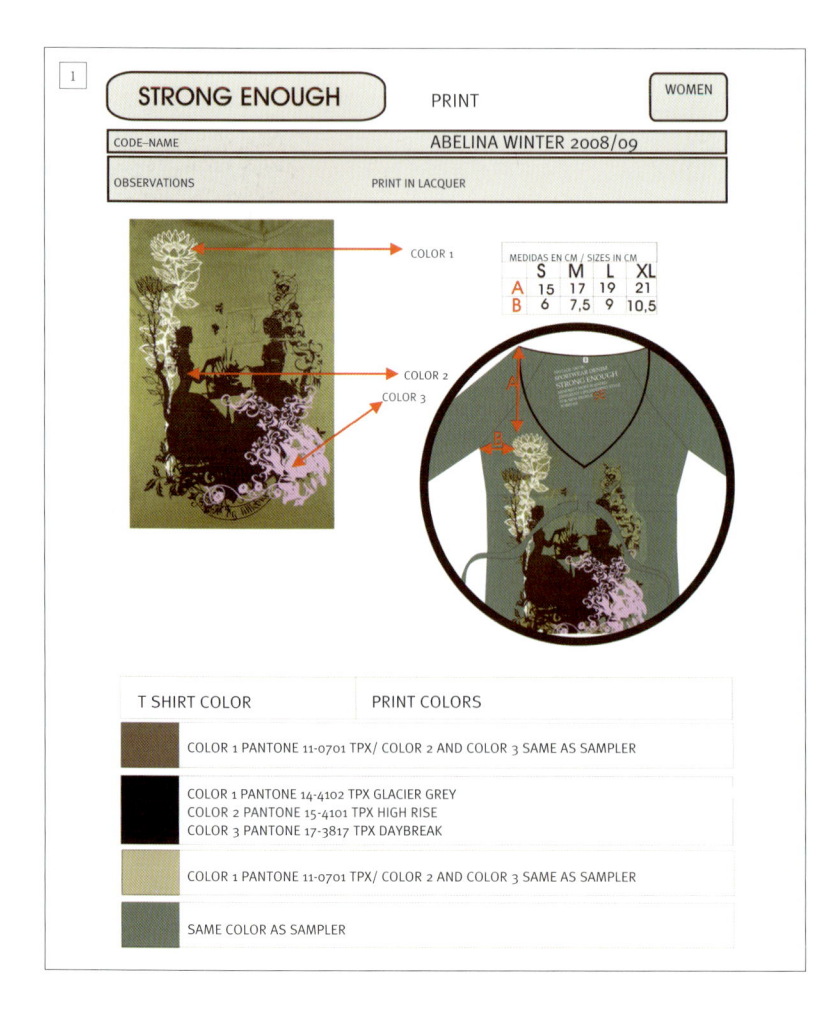

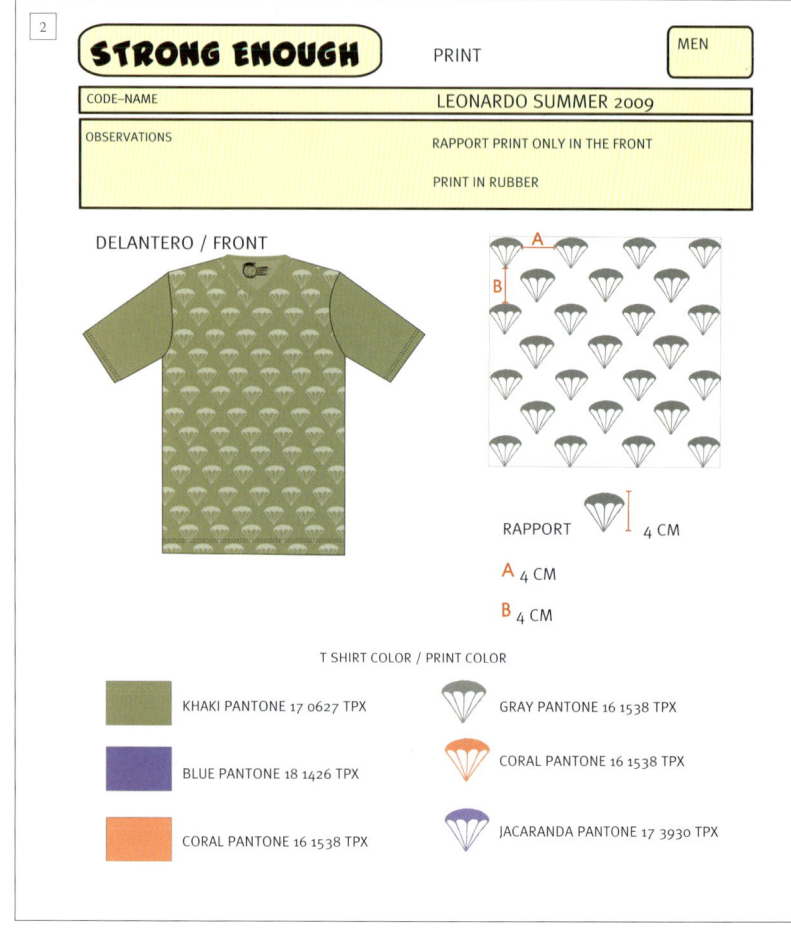

positional printing and rapport **65**

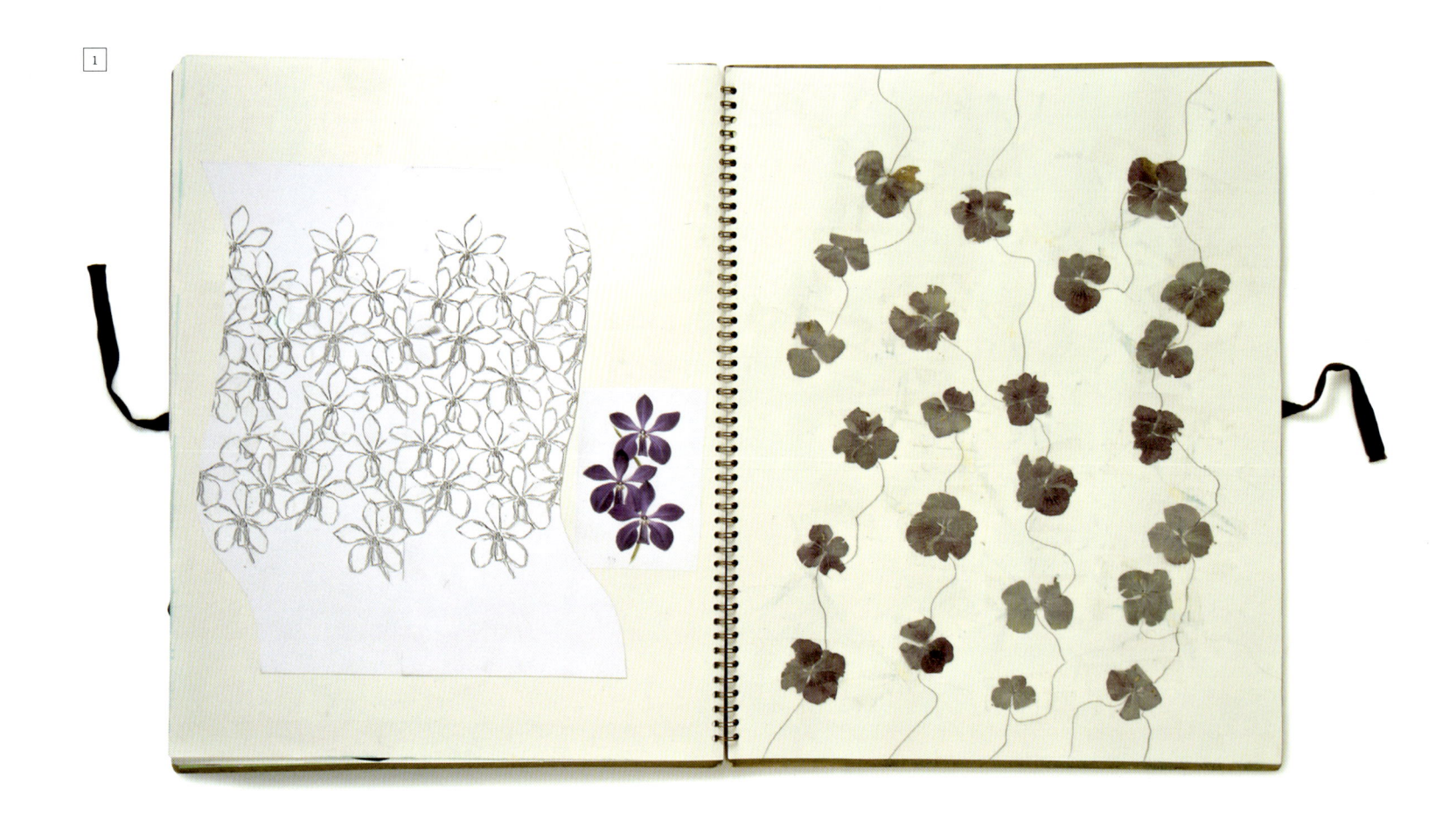

1. Sketchbook collage by Javier Nanclares created using photocopies, photo of main motif, and dry flowers.

2. Drawing with felt-tip pen and motif drawn with black line.

3. Drawing with colored pencils that reflect the interior of the flower made separately to create a weaving texture.

4. Once drawings 2 and 3 are scanned a composition is made digitally to obtain a continuous print.

66 FROM THE IDEA TO THE PRODUCT: the technical process

5. Continuous print for masculine underwear by Laura Fernández. From the Giulio company.

6. Heraldry-inspired drawing for positional print in underwear garment. From the Giulio company.

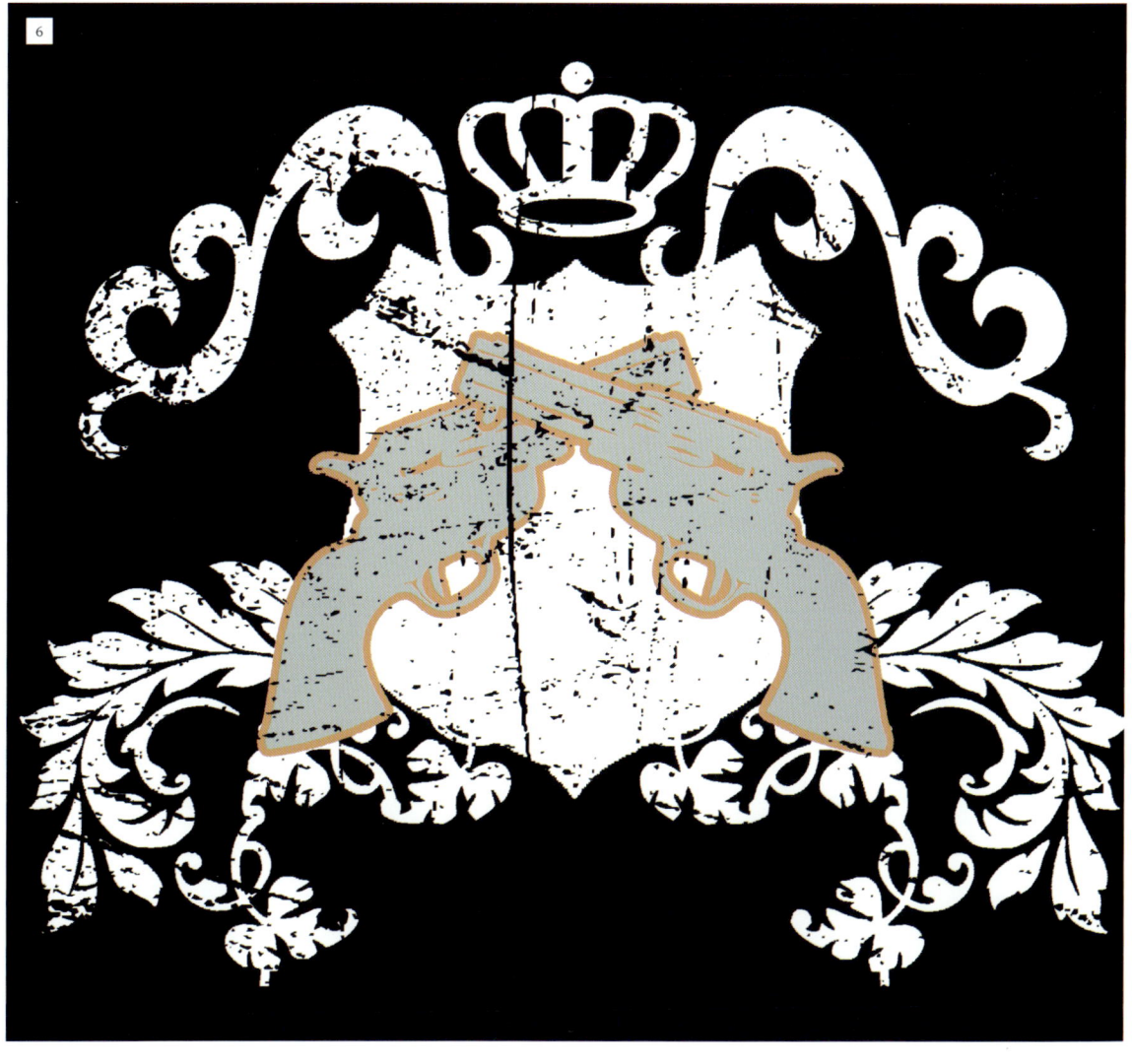

positional printing and rapport **67**

1-2-3. Paola Ivana Suhonen's designs, from the same inspirational source (animals), are applied to the garments as continuous prints.

4-5-6-7. The same Bambi theme has been developed in different prints. The one that has the underlying rhombuses is a rapport, and the one with the border around the motif is positional. By Paola Ivana Suhonen. Collection Spring-Summer 2008.

68 FROM THE IDEA TO THE PRODUCT: the technical process

positional printing and rapport 69

THE RAPPORT TECHNIQUE

Rapport is the basic module of repetition of a motif or design for the creation of a patterned printing. In other words, it is the basic unit of the design that extends in all directions of the fabric. This composition is carried out from a specific design that is reformulated to obtain optimum repetition.

There are different methods for creating a continuous design, but the most commonly used is made with a computer. To achieve this, the motif is first placed in the center of the working document. Afterwards a copy is placed to the right, and another to the left of the central motif, forming a diagonal line.

The next step involves copying that diagonal above and under the central line. This way, a graphic module is generated (with the motif copied nine times) that will lay the foundations for the repetition in all directions.

1. Base motif drawn by hand.

2. The scanned base motif is repeated in a diagonal line towards the right to give the composition rhythm.

3. The same operation is performed towards the left, following the diagonal towards the opposite side until it forms an inclined line wit h three motifs.

4. The inclined line of three motifs doubles in the top part.

5. The inclined line of three motifs is repeated in the bottom part. Now, you've obtained the complete floral design.

positional printing and rapport **71**

TECHNIQUES

Either through craft methods or through the use of digital technologies, designers have a wide variety of techniques with which to represent their fabric creations. In fact, any image, whether an illustration or a photograph, is most likely going to be subject to some material-specific procedures. In addition, the results obtained will always be different from the designer's original concept.

One of the most common techniques is screenprinting, a technique especially recommended for flat or plotted colors. This method of printing offers very different effects with respect to the quality of color and textures.

In turn, embroidery, with its wide variety of threads and techniques, is another frequently used resource. It can be manual or machine made. In this latter case, a computer program performs a series of actions selected according to the designer's illustration.

Another great technique is digital printing, which transfers information to an inkjet printer to display every type of image with great definition. The advantage of the digital process over the traditional one is that it allows passing directly from the design to the printing, without having to prepare movies and shablones. This latter procedure is the most frequently used in rapport prints. The technique that is selected depends on the effect that the designer looks for. Many times a combination of different techniques provides the best results.

1-2. Screenprinting and embroidery of sequins in silk chiffon are part of the same pattern of development.

72 APPLICATION OF THE DESIGNS TO FABRIC: the final result

3. Original illustration with motifs of animals before printing on the final garment. By Miriam Ocáriz. Collection Spring-Summer 2008.

1

2

1. Original hand drawing made with linoleum on paper.

2. Lithograph on paper.

3. Manipulated digital image.

4. Handkerchief in silk chiffon, digital impression. By Javier Nanclares.

74 FROM THE IDEA TO THE PRODUCT: the technical process

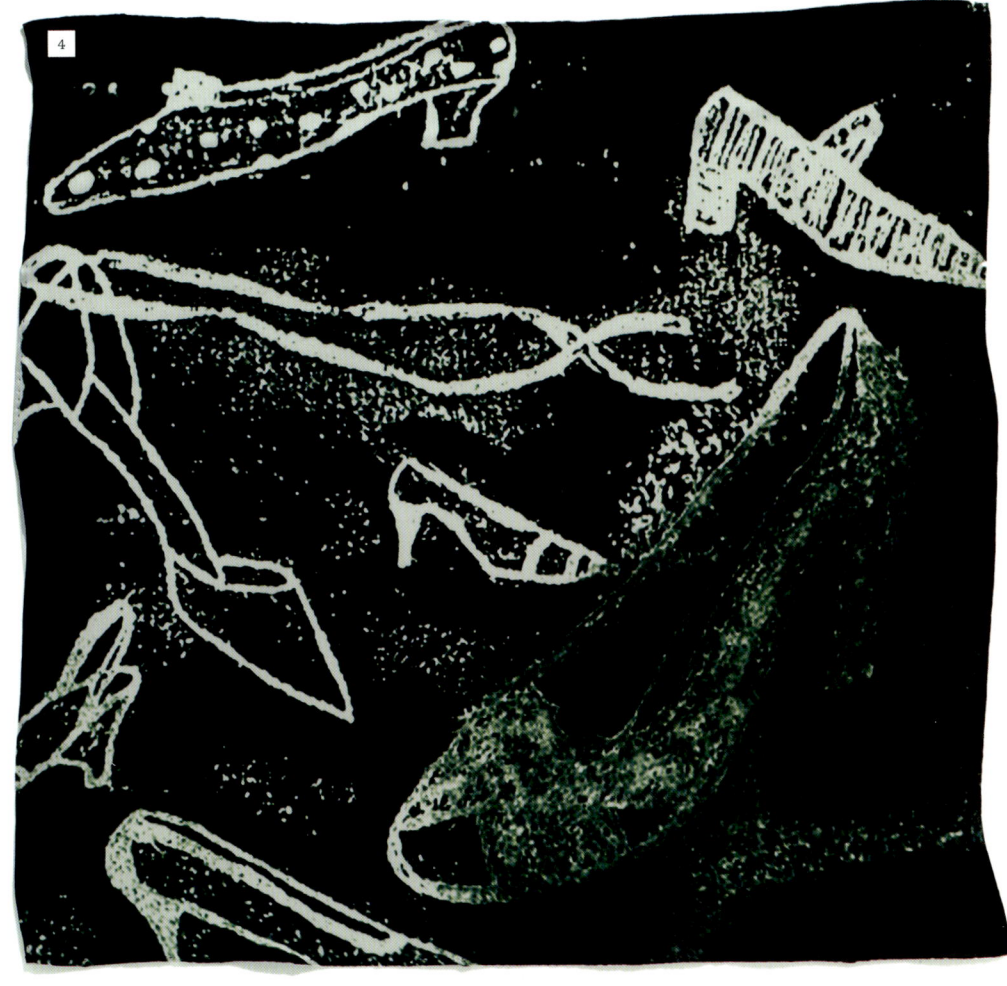

techniques of use 75

APPLYING THE DESIGNS TO FABRIC
the final result

RAW MATERIAL

To obtain the best results of the textiles selected by the customer or to highlight the printing, the designer must know the raw materials in depth. At present, the continuous research on new materials and the demands of the market make the textile industry one of the most dynamic and changing sectors. The most important lines of innovation are in the new fibers, membranes, processes, and treatments, in which biotechnology and nanotechnology provide functional properties to the textile materials.

Besides the technical characteristics of the fabrics, the designers must be attentive to the trends that appear in the sector of the market that their creations are destined for. For example, the increasing consciousness of the need to take care of the environment makes more designers and brands decide to use sustainable fabrics in their dressmaking.

The names of the fabrics indicate the method used to intertwine the threads and not the fiber that they contain. At first, some fabrics were only associated with the fiber that was used, as it happened with taffeta or satin (made of silk), twill (a crossed fabric limited in the past to wool), or denim, originally made only of cotton. Today, they produce taffeta from nylon, satin from cotton, twill from silk, and denim from mixed fibers.

The common fabric—called smooth, or taffeta, fabric—is composed of two perpendicular series of threads: the warp, which goes in a longitudinal direction, and the weft, which goes in a transverse direction, in which each of their units receives the name of the last.

Other variations of smooth fabric include intermeshed and fluted. The crossed fabric, in turn, is characterized by the very marked, diagonal lines caused by the intertwining of two threads of the warp with a thread of the weft in alternate rows. This effect can be observed in fabrics such as twill, gabardine, or denim.

Satins have a texture denser than the crossed fabrics, but their main characteristics are smoothness and endurance. The soft surface of the fabric of satin is achieved by passing the threads of the warp on some threads of the weft with minimum intertwining; the reflection of the light in the free threads produces its characteristic brightness. The best known are crepe satin, silk satin, and damask.

The harness and jacquard systems are used to fabricate materials with drawings, such as brocades, whereas fabrics with a pile, like velvet, felt, corduroy and plush, are fabricated combining smooth fabric with the use of wires that take out additional threads of the weft or the warp and form loops in the fabric. In the plush, the loops are not cut, unlike what occurs with velvet.

There are also textiles that are not woven, whose structure is achieved by joining or intertwining fibers with mechanical, chemical, or thermal methods, using solvents or combining the previous methods.

The appearance of the prints is different, depending on the fiber, the weft, and the finishing of the fabric. The same drawing on a light gauze of fine and transparent thread will acquire another character on an opaque fabric of thicker texture and brightness, such as satin. Even if both fabrics are carried out in silk, and they both have been printed with the same procedure and coloring, the effect will be different when using a base with different transparency, texture, and brightness. Because of this, it is very important to identify the textile fibers and the way in which they affect the printing and influence the final result. The chart on page 82 lists the different fibers with which the industry works.

The same print has been applied to garments of different materials: silk knitting (1), gauze (2) and satin (3).

4. Original drawing for print from the Miriam Ocáriz company. Fall-Winter Collection 2008-2009.

5. The weight and the texture of the fabric define new dimensions in prints.

Initially, any fabric will be suitable for decoration by printing or applique and embroidery. Their composition does not pose a problem when they merely serve as a base for the initial designs. However, the correct choice of fabric can be important later on, depending on the final effect, which the designer wants to obtain.

For more complex handwork, such as batik, cotton or silk is generally used. To paint manually, the most popular technique is painting on silk, but it is also common to use other bases and techniques to obtain very different and creative works.

Because screenprinting is a superficial application—the same as sewing, embroideries, and applications—it is suitable for all materials. Knitwear and elastics, in turn, can be used for transfers or printing, as the inks are elastic nowadays and penetrate into the fabric to adapt to the great market of the knitting fashion. Only in the case of the sublimation, or devoré, technique is there a need to use a fabric with a percentage of polyester.

THE FIBERS

Fibers that come from natural sources can be of a vegetable (composed of cellulose) or animal (composed of proteins) nature. Chemical fibers, in turn, can be artificial, made from the transformation of natural polymers, such as cellulose, or synthetic, manufactured from polymers obtained industrially from derivatives of oil.

1. Presentation of the selection of fabrics with the prototypes of garments, for the collection by Syngman Cucala.

2. Applied on a fabric of brilliant fibers. In it the colors of this design stand out in a special way (WGSN).

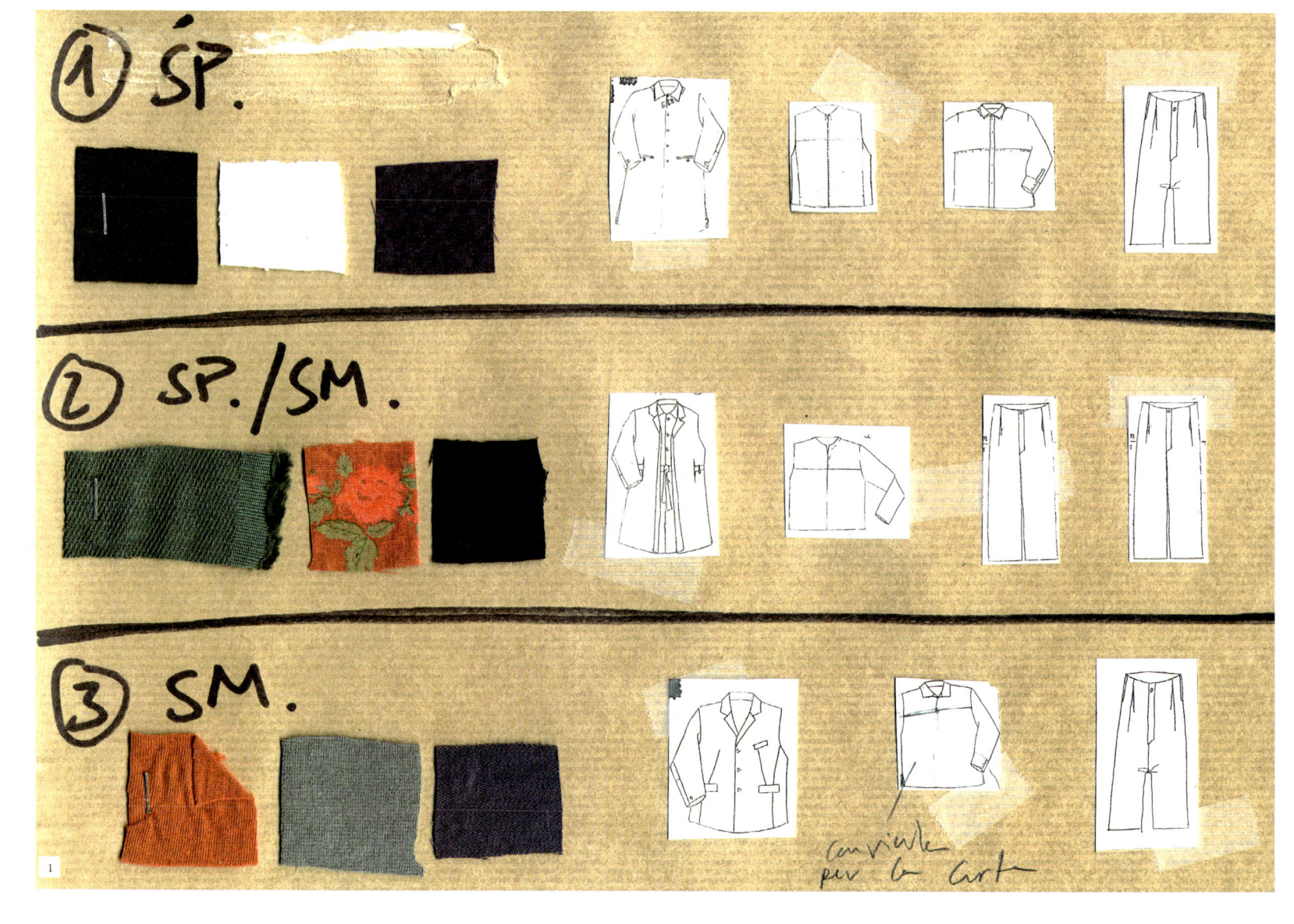

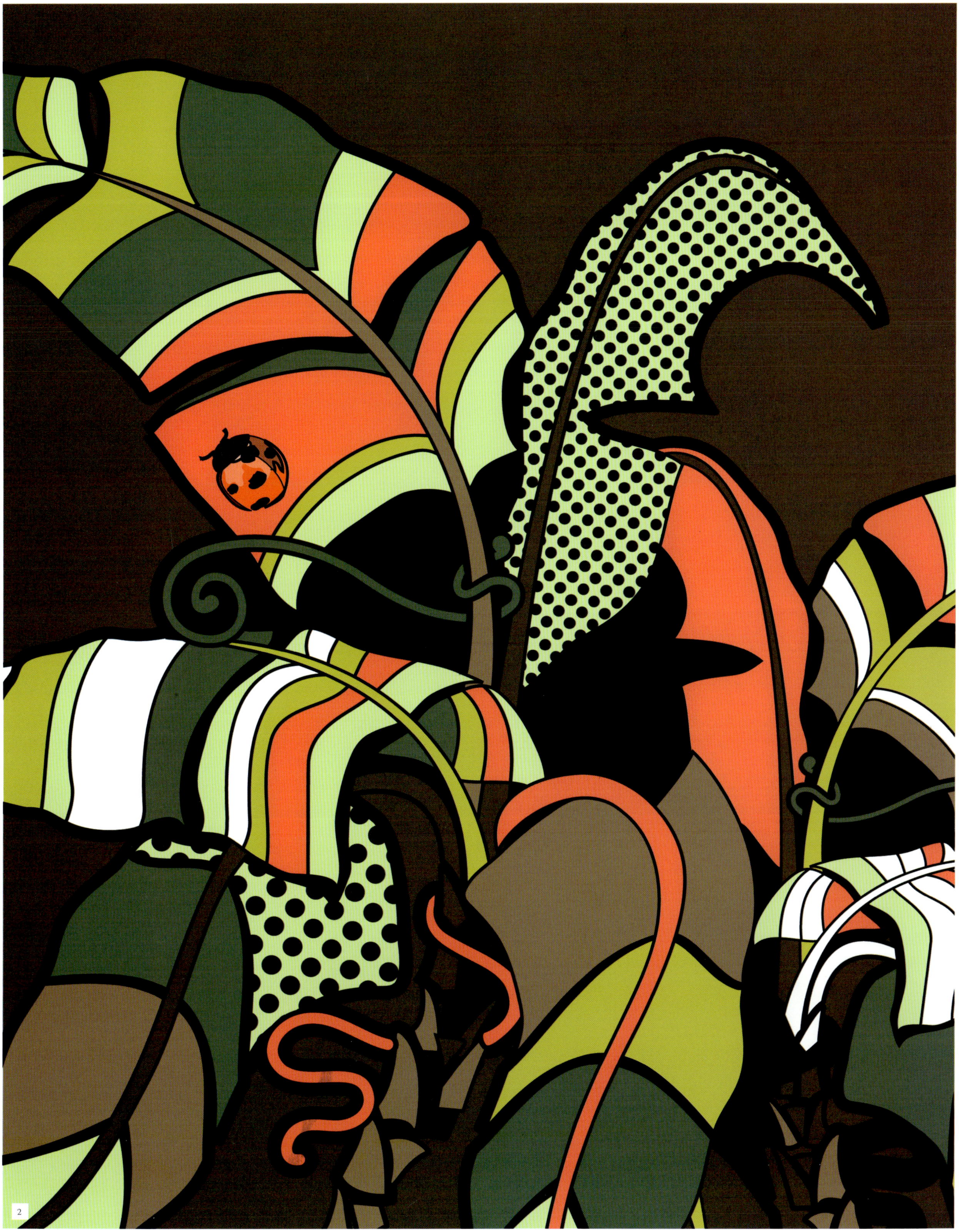

2

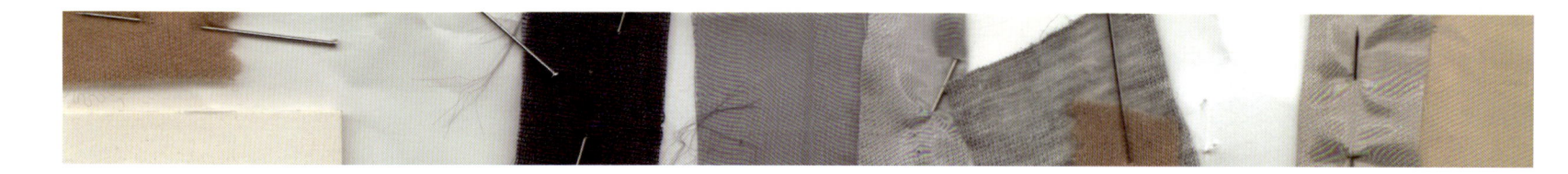

GENEALOGY OF FIBERS

WOOLS: SHEEP (MERINO, SHETLAND, LAMBSWOOL)

HORSE: HORSE (MANE AND TAIL) | BULL | AMERICAN CAMELIDAE (ALPACA, LLAMA, VICUNA, GUANACO) | GOAT (MOHAIR, CASHMERE, TIBET) | RABBIT (DOMESTIC, ANGORA) | HARE (HAIR OF HARE) | CAMEL (BABY CAMEL) - DROMEDARY

SILK: SILK WORM (BOMBYX MORI: FROM THE COCOON OF THE WORM) (TUSSAH: WILD SILK)

ANIMALS

SEED OR FRUIT: COTTON | COCONUT | KAPOK | ASCLEPIAS

STEM: LINEN | JUTE | RAMIE | URENA | GINESTA OR BROOM | ROSELLA (MALLOW)

HEMP: SUNN (INDIAN HEMP) | KENAF (HEMP OF GUINEA)

LEAF: FIQUE | ESPARTO | ABACA | FORMIO | RAFFIA ALBARDIN | PALM | SISAL (LEAF OF THE AGAVE) | SISAL (AGAVE SISALANA) | PITA (AMERICAN AGAVE)

VEGETABLES

NATURALS: GLASS (FIBERGLASS, ISOLAM)

TRANSFORMED: GOLD | SILVER | COPPER | LAME-LUREX | MELTON

MINERALS

NATURAL FIBERS (DISCONTINUOUS)

82 APPLYING THE DESIGNS TO FABRIC: the final result

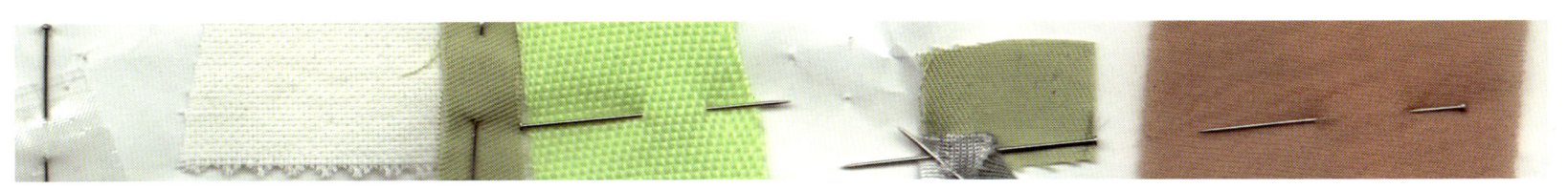

Selección de tejidos para colección de Hamish Morrow.

(1-2) PROTEINS (VEGETABLE OR ANIMAL ALBUMIN)
CASEIN (MERINOVA, FROM THE CASEIN OF MILK) | LEGUMES (ARDIL, PEANUT, VICARA, CORN, SOY, SOY GRAINS)

(1) CELLULOSE (REGENERATED, MODIFIED)
VISCOSE (VISCOUS RAYON, FIBRIN RAYON, CUPRAMMONIUM RAYON) | PAPER (WITH SODA OR SULPHITE) | CELLULOSE ESTERS (DIACETATE-DICEL, TRIACETATE-TRICEL ARNEL, TRILAN, TRIACETATE OF CELLULOSE) | ACETATE (CELLULOSE ACETATE-RAYON ACETATE)

(1) ALGINIC
ALGINATES | SEAWEEDS

(1) RUBBER AND GUM
GUM (FROM THE EXTRUDED LATEX FOR EXTRUSION (ROUND SECTION) OR FROM RUBBER LEAVES (SQUARE SECTION)

ARTIFICIAL (FOR DISSOLUTION) NATURAL POLYMERS OF VEGETABLE (1) OR ANIMAL (2) ORIGIN

CHLOROFIBERS
OF POLYVINYL (RHOVYL-MOVYL) | OF POLYVINYLIDENE CHLORIDE (SARAN)

POLYAMIDES
NYLON 6 (PERLON., ENKALON) | NYLON 6-6 (NYLON) | NYLON II (RILSAN) | NYLON HT (NOMEX)

POLYESTER
TERGAL | TERLENKA

ACRYLIC
PURE (OURON, DRALON, LEACRIL, COURTELLE) | MODIFIED (DYNEL)

OIL-BASED
POLYETHYLENE | POLYPROPYLENE (MERCLON)

VINYL
ALCOHOL OF POLYVINYL (KURALON)

POLYURETHANE
LYCRA | SPANDEX

FLUOROCARBONS
TEFLON

SYNTHETIC (FOR REACTION) SYNTHETIC POLYMERS

CHEMICAL FIBERS (CONTINUOUS)

raw material **83**

SPINNING

Fibers are processed through spinning to convert them into what will be used to weave, sew, and embroider. The industrial spinning technique is complex and it changes with constant technological advances. It is adapted with great speed to the trends and demands of the market with respect to coloring, quality, and finishes.

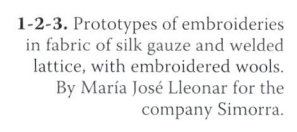

1-2-3. Prototypes of embroideries in fabric of silk gauze and welded lattice, with embroidered wools. By María José Lleonar for the company Simorra.

4-5-6-7. Four different models with printed dresses. Collection Fall-Winter 2006/2007. By Josep Font.

84 APPLYING THE DESIGNS TO FABRIC: the final result

raw material 85

FABRICS

From a technical point of view, fabric is the name given to the material obtained in the form of a sheet more or less resistant, elastic, and flexible, through the crossing and linking of two series of threads, one longitudinal and another transversal.

It is composed of a warp, which are the threads that go in the longitudinal direction (thread), and a weft, which are the threads that are intertwined in the transverse direction (last). Depending on its structure, they are classified as fabrics of plane or of sunk type, knitwear, and fabrics that are not woven.

FABRICS OF PLANE OR SUNK TYPE
These types of fabrics are defined in part from the method of construction:

- **SATIN** is woven so the warp remains above the weft, or vice versa. This characteristic creates a soft, smooth and shining aspect on the front of the fabric, and a matte back.

- **TAFFETA** presents a cross that is simpler, with a similar thickness of threads. The thread of the warp, and that of the weft, passes in alternatively. An equally thick and smooth fabric is obtained on both sides, and there is not a front or back.

- **SERGE** presents a gradual structure with an oblique arrangement. The fabric has a front and back, and is characterized by strong resistance. The fabric most characteristic of this technique is denim.

KNITWEAR
These are the fabrics that form with at least one thread that is intertwined to itself. Hand knitting is done with two needles: one does the knitting and the other holds the fabric that is continually formed. From this technique derives knitting with machinery, where the material is built by intertwining loops of lines of thread in transverse and longitudinal directions. This composition is the one that provides the fabric with its characteristic elasticity. At the horizontal rows, it designates the weft last, at the vertical columns. In this case, the texture and the drawing are obtained through the use of several needles, threads, colors, or the selection of different knitwear. The designs in the knitted goods are also achieved by embroidery and the techniques of screenprinting.

WELDED LATTICES
Fabrics with metallic yarns are continuously in fashion. Originally they came from threads of gold or of silver, although at present, the more commonly used fabrics are steel, aluminum, iron, nickel, or alloys with cobalt. They can be of sunk type as well as of knitting.

WOVEN FABRICS THAT ARE NOT WOVEN
Fabrics that are not woven also are used in fashion, for sport footwear, linings, cushion fillings, and accessories. Generally they are strong and resistant, and because of their construction, they do not fray or break easily. These fabrics are obtained by compressing fibers and then applying heat, friction, or chemical products. One of the best known is felt. DuPont is one of the more prestigious manufacturers in the development of products made of this type of material.

SKIN AND LEATHER
Thanks to the beauty of their fur, many animals are bred in farms to use their skins in fashion. For the textile designer, this is a very interesting resource, since the skins can be dyed with drawings, cut, and manipulated with ornaments and embroidery.

Additionally, strips of skin can be woven, creating a new texture, and bits of skin can be included in collages. Leather can also generate a great quantity of effects with completed dyes, textures, and cutbacks, creating patent leathers and fantastic imitations of exotic skins, such as that of snake or crocodile. The use of animal skins today is very much a controversial subject. Nowadays, this industry is totally legislated, therefore the animals destined for fashion are reared and killed under specific conditions.

PLASTICS
Plastics are not natural products. They are obtained through different chemical reactions to which an additive is incorporated. The results are called polymers. These fibers constitute the base of the plasticized fabrics, generally used in the designs of rain or fantasy wear.

1-2-3. Print to be applied on flexible fabrics that adapt to the form of the body. From Lisa Italia. Winter Collection 2008.

4-5. Samples of vinyls (PVC) with colors, textures, and prints.

6. Samples of skins with fur (astrakhan, ermine, mink, mouton) and imitation leathers with texture of snake and embossed floral print.

raw material 87

TYPES OF FABRICS

Sight and touch are the best means for recognizing the different types of textiles. Here are some of the most widely used among hundreds of different qualities, which vary and change constantly as the industry progresses. Still, they always conserve their title in reference to their traditional name.

ACETATE. Chemical silk (artificial fiber) obtained from cellulose acetate was discovered in Germany in 1869. Since 1920, this fiber has been used in the manufacture of lingerie, blouses, dresses, and knitwear, as well as other garments requiring light and delicate fabrics. It is strong and easy to maintain, with no shrinking, wrinkling, or fading. Washed under 104° F (40° C) and dried in the shade.

ALPACA. Material made of woven fibers of alpaca wool; used especially in making men's clothing.

BATISTE. Named in honor of its creator, Baptiste Cambray (a thirteenth-century French weaver). Batiste is a very fine fabric of linen or cotton, bleached in part, slightly prepared, and hot-pressed. It is used for pocket handkerchiefs, dresses, and shirts.

BROCADE. Sumptuous silk fabric made on a jacquard loom. Threads of gold or silver form part of the fabric (no embroidery), with relief, as well as drawings, with floral and arabesque motifs. It is used mainly in church ornaments and gowns.

CHIFFON. Fabric of silk or a synthetic fiber, very light and brilliant (with the appearance of gauze), woven with light fibers, but with twisted thread.

CHINTZ. Fabric originating in India, made of shiny cotton, and printed in bright colors.

CALICO. From Calicut, the city in India from which it was first imported. An inexpensive, plain, white, unprinted cotton cloth.

CORDUROY. The velvet weft. The warp and weft form the base fabric and the other weft, the rought cut, shapes the characteristic feel of this fabric. Usually woven of cotton, but also with rayon. Corduroy can also be smooth, square, and adorned. Traditionally, corduroy of brown or black color was the typical fabric of peasants. Manufactured in all colors and a wide variety of thicknesses, today it also comes in a variety of weights.

COTELINE. Ribbed fabric made of wool or cotton. Used formerly for suits, jackets, blazers, and coats.

COTTON. Vegetable fiber that is separated from the seeds (which it covers) of the cotton plant. The quality of cotton depends on its fineness, purity, brilliance, and, above all, the length of the fiber; the older it is, the thinner, more resistant, and more regular is the thread that is produced. Linens and bedding are made from short cotton fiber cuts. Long fibers are used for batiste fabrics, poplin, and damask. This fiber is highly absorbent, resistant to heat, washable, and impervious to moths. It is not compressible, nor does it accrue static electricity. Untreated, it is used to make wadding.

CREPE. Fabrics made of silk, linen, and cotton, which have a wrinkly surface.

CREPE GEORGETTE. Very lightweight and transparent fabric; matte and soft to the touch.

CRESPÓN. Thin and wrinkled fabric that is produced by twisting many of the warp and weft threads. It is made in wool, silk, cotton, rayon, linen, and also in combinations. It is usually printed and used a lot in women's clothing.

CRETONNE. Cotton fabric printed in colors, on which flowers are the typical pattern. It is a strong fabric that is used mainly for curtains and upholstery.

DAMASK. Originally a figured fabric of silk or linen with designs worked into the fabric, showing a shiny pattern on one side and the same inverted design on the other. Fabrics of cotton, rayon, wool, or blends in a jacquard-style fabric are also known as damask.

DENIM. The fabric of all cowboy fashion. It entered the fashion world in the 1940s. A twilled fabric made of cotton, very resistant, easy to wash, and very hard-wearing.

FELT. Textile product obtained without weaving. Manufactured by making the properties of certain fibers—especially wool—interlace and cling together. These properties are encouraged by the friction of the fibers in a water-based medium with pressure and heat.

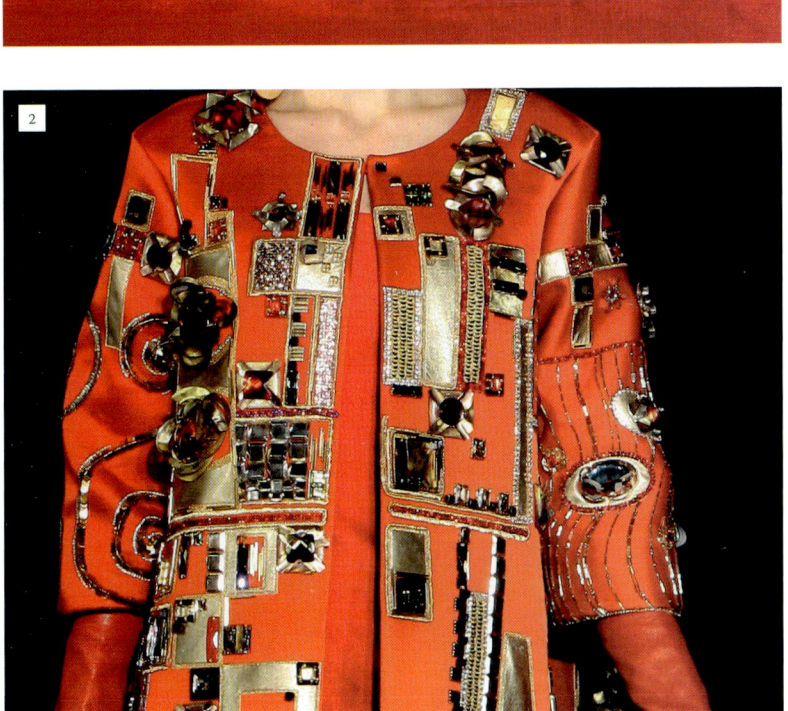

1. Embroidery with silk threads on chantung of natural silk of the collection by the designer Manuel Albarrán.

2. Prints with applications of stones and metallic pieces. By Christian Dior. Collection Spring-Summer 2008.

3. Print of leopard on fabric of silk. By Christian Dior.

FLANNEL. Generic name for several woolen fabrics that have in common a simple or cross weft. They are smooth to the touch, because the finish is combed on one side. When made with thin threads of wool, it is used for coats and suits, and with cotton, raising one or both sides, for indoor clothing such as pajamas and shirts. Flannelette, which is a lighter and softer material, is always made of combed cotton.

GABARDINE. A closely woven twill fabric. It also has artificial fibers and different thicknesses. Since 1902, gabardine has been a trademark registered by Burberry.

GAUZE. Probably from Arabic Gazza (silk), or from Gaza, Palestine. A thin, lightly woven, transparent silk material used for transparent blouses, dresses, and scarves. There is also a cotton gauze that has a very loose weave and is heavily treated.

GEORGETTE. Very fine and transparent crepe that is made from highly heavily threads.

GLACILLA. Fabric used in tests before using the original fabric.

GROSGRAIN. Special fabric for ribbons of silk, rayon, or cotton, which is horizontally fluted.

GUIPURE. Thick lace embroidered with a motif with a background of ties or thick thread.

JERSEY. Fine knitwear created on the island of Jersey (United Kingdom). Can be manufactured from various textile materials on warp or weft circular knitting machines or straight machines.

LAMINA (LAMÉ). Sumptuous fabrics that have fancy threads of gold or silver interwoven into them. Used in dresses and ballgowns.

LINEN. A cloth made from flax fiber whose threads frequently have an irregularity of thickness. The fabric is fine and strong, but it does not have easy-care properties.

LYCRA. Chemical fiber based on elastomers of polyurethane, manufactured exclusively by the company Du Pont (Delaware, USA.). Elastic, resistant to fire and humidity, and holds its shape. It is an essential component of undergarments and some sportswear. When it is mixed with other fabrics, it adds elasticity to the weave.

MADRAS. Cloth that has been exported from India to the West for more than a century. It is a light, open fabric made of cotton, woven by hand, dyed with vegetable dyes, and hand printed with patterns and motifs of the maker's country of origin.

MATTE. This term refers to many fabrics of cotton or linen. In embroidery, it refers to the stage when the weft is very visible, and it is regulated by positioning each point or cutting the openwork with precision (Hardanger). There are different sizes designated by a figure that corresponds to the number of weft threads per centimeter or per inch (2.54 centimeters).

MOHAIR. Fabric made from hair of the Angora goat or by mixing this with cotton, wool, or silk. It always has a side of frayed hair.

MOIRE. Fabric, usually of silk, whose thick silk weft, schappe, or cotton makes horizontal cords, also known as fay. It is referred to as watered silk because its main feature is the optical effect that occurs in the form of wavy reflections, or water, which change according to the incidence of light shining on it.

MUSLIN. Fabric originally from Mussul (Iraq). It arrived in Western Europe in the 17th century, and, in the 18th, began to be manufactured in England and France. In the 1960s, it was especially popular for dresses of hippie fashion. It is a lightweight, translucent, woven cotton that can range from soft to the touch, to coarse.

ORGANDY. Fabric made from cotton, with very fine and regular threads. Two important features of organdy are its semi-transparency and rigidity, which reappear when ironing the fabric after washing. It is a fine, thin muslin.

PERCALE. From the Persian *pargale*. A smooth, closely woven, lightweight material usually made of cotton. Similar to cretonne but of a better, finer, and higher density. Can be bleached, dyed in part, or, more generally, printed. Frequently used for bed linens.

PIQUÉ. Stiff, corded fabric generally woven from cotton, which has geometric patterns on it. More commonly, it is made of materials with two sides, or double-sided fabric, leading to drawings that are more or less geometrical in relief. The material is often bleached, although it is sometimes dyed in light colors.

PLUSH. A kind of velvet, though it has a longer and more open pile than ordinary velvet. Generally, the pile is composed of wool or cotton made up of the warp threads. It's called plush long hair when the pile is 0.4 inches (1cm) in length.

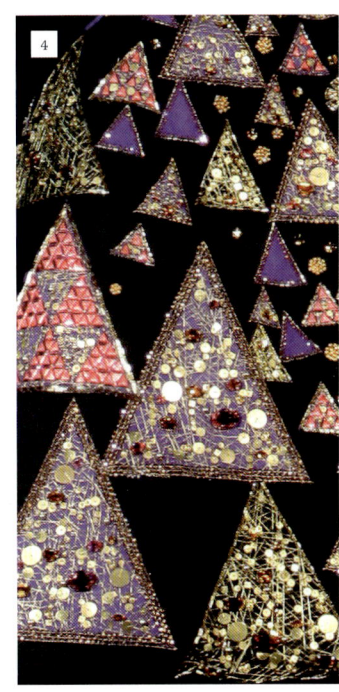

1. Taffeta of silk with hand embroidery.

2. Embroidery, with metallic threads and applications, on silk taffeta. By Christian Dior. Spring/Summer 2008 collection.

3. Silk chiffon dress with floral print. Spring-summer 2009 (Première Vision Paris).

4. Silk taffeta dress with geometrical motifs and sequins embroidered on it. By Christian Dior. Spring/summer 2008.

POPLIN. Strong fabric that was first manufactured in Avignon, when this city was the papal seat. It is possible that its name derives from that time. Currently, poplin is made in combed and mercerized cotton, or in blends of cotton, silk, wool, and artificial and synthetic fibers. It is a very durable material, used especially for shirts and blouses.

SATIN. The name might have the same Latin origin of silk, or may be originally from a town in China, where a very thick and shining fabric of silk was woven. Now, it is also made from rayon, the fabric often replacing silk. It is a luxury fabric for wedding gowns, formal dresses, or nightwear.

SILK SATIN. Silk fabric with warp of silk or mercerized cotton and weft of other fibers, always with a smooth and lustrous surface, for the effect of a silk-like material.

SHANTUNG. Fabric formerly made with greige silk, which was spun in Shantung, China. Now, it is also made of cotton and rayon. It is known as a fabric or wild silk with varying thicknesses presented in the form of flames.

SPANDEX. Fabric of the fiber of the same name. Very elastic; used for stockings, corsetry, and swimwear.

TAFFETA. From the Persian *tâftah*, which means spinning, and *täfteh*, meaning brilliant. Thick fabric made of fine threads of silk or slightly stiff cotton. Has a crisp feel, like silk, and has an iridescent appearance.

TULLE. First appeared in Tulle, France, in the mid-18th century. Originally done by hand, it is a stiffened, sheer net made of silk or cotton. Today, it is made on special looms.

TWEED. Woven wool fabric of bulky and strong appearance, originally produced by hand in homes in southern Scotland. Today, this name refers to tweeds manufactured on the loom, usually of wool, though sometimes with a bit of cotton added in.

VELOUR. From the French word for velvet. Items presently known as velour have a surface imitating silk velvet knitted from synthetic fibers. It is used for trim and decoration.

VELVET. Fabric with a short, thick, and perpendicular pile. Initially made of silk, and later of rayon, this fabric is often associated with luxury.

VICHY. A fine cotton fabric with threads of bright and solid colors, forming simple drawings (lists and tables). Used for gowns for women, common linen and shirts for men.

WAXED. Ribbon or strong fabric with a glossy wax finish.

1-2. Original design applied to both silk gauze and satin silk, which makes evident the difference in transparency and brightness obtained on each surface. From SIMORRA.

raw material **93**

94 APPLYING THE DESIGNS TO FABRIC: the final result

1-2. Floral designs on muslin. From the company Miriam Ocáriz.

DYES, VARNISHES, AND PIGMENTS

Dye is a substance pigmented with a density that can range from liquid to viscose. Its components are the pigment, or dye, known as coloring; the binding, also called the vehicle, which is the heavy medium in which the pigment is dispersed; and other additives, such as stabilizers, solvents, and softeners. The dyes most frequently used are:

PLASTISOL OR ACRYLIC VARNISHES. Known for their shininess and elasticity. They are also very durable and resistant to washing.
BLEACHES. Ideal for whitening natural fabrics, discoloring already dyed fabrics, or obtaining the effects of being cleaned with bleach and aged.
BASE COLORS. Applied on dark fabrics.
GLUE. Self-adhesive plastisol used for achieving various effects, for example: crimson, velvet, caviar (gluing small beads), glitter, metallics, etc.
INKS WITH SPECIAL EFFECTS. Metallized (gold, silver, bronze, copper) luminous, aged, glitter, and pearly.
VARNISHES FOR FLOCKING. Inflatable dyes.
DYES OF HIGH DENSITY. Used for prints requiring high relief.
NATURAL DYES AND ORGANIC PIGMENT. Extracted from plants, animals, and minerals. Currently, there is renewed interest in their use, with all the concern about environmental issues.
WATER-BASED DYES. There are different variants for natural, mixed, or synthetic blend fabrics. They are suitable for plain fabrics.

1. Cans of paint with color reference numbers in a screenprinting workshop.

2. Although workshops have computer programs to decide on the composition of various colors, often they resort to mixing the colors by hand with a special scale.

3. Drawing prepared in layers for the screenprinting workshop. The textile designer indicates the colors that compose the drawing: the first is the background color (that of the fabric), and for the other five, a layer of color is applied to each. The workshop, therefore, should prepare five dyes or varnishes with the color desired, and five screens—one for each color.

4. A blank silk-screen, formed by a frame with a fabric, on which an emulsion will be applied, tautly stretched over it. Originally, these screens were made of silk. Today, there are other, stronger materials that allow reuse of the screens.

5. Ultraviolet light used in the screenprinting process. Once the emulsion is applied to the screen (see p. 102), the screen is subjected to a light that fixes the design onto the screen.

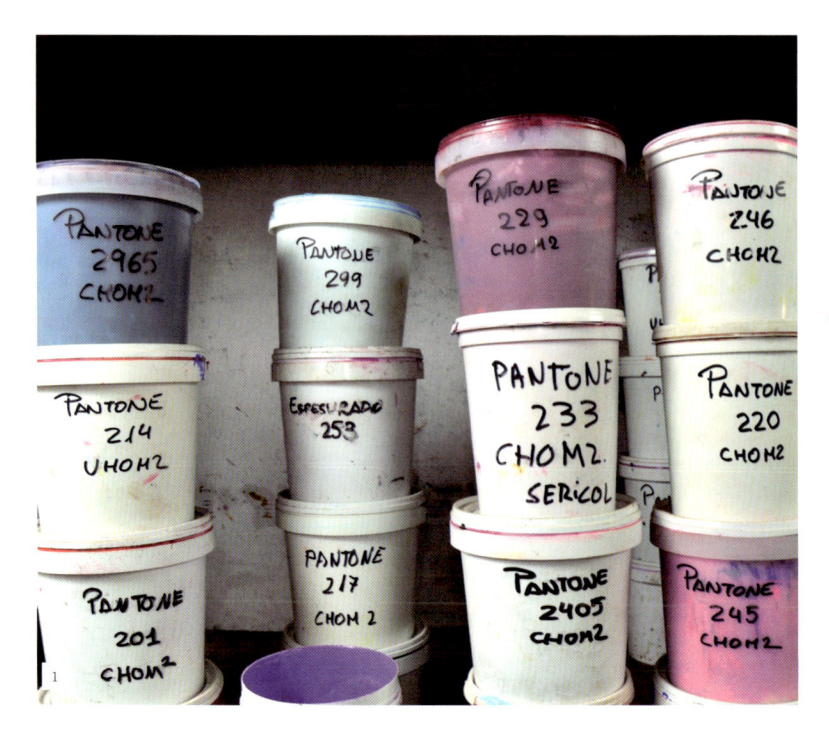

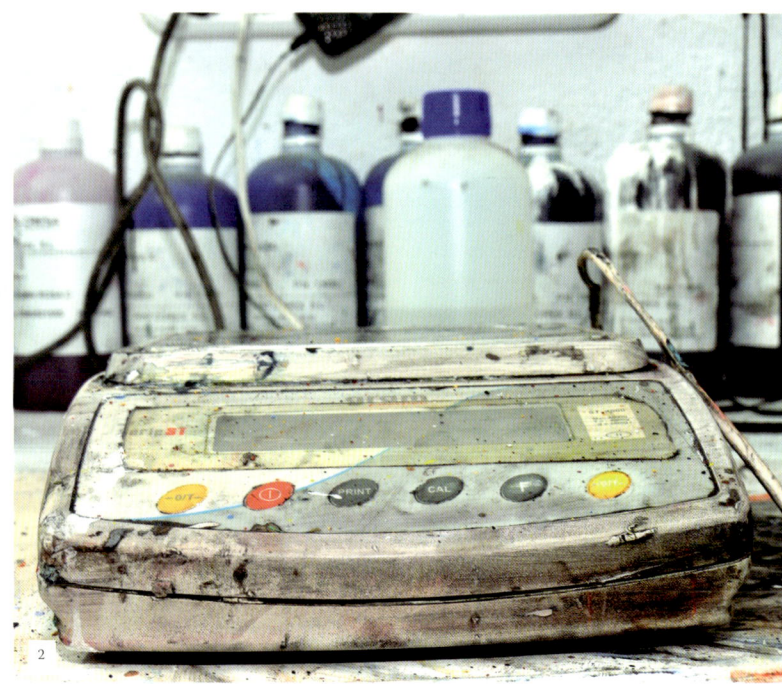

96 APPLYING THE DESIGNS TO FABRIC: the final result

	Col 1: ground		Col 2: softhand print		Col 3: softhand print		Col 4: softhand print
▢	Col. 210 milky petrol	■	Col. 920 anthra	▢	Col. 710 berry	■	Col. plum

	Col 5: softhand print		Col 6: softhand print		
▢	Col. sporty green	▢	Col. 530 oak	•	Crystals

dyes, varnishes, and pigments 97

FINAL PRINTING PROCESSES

Printing is the process by which the coloration of a fabric, according to preconceived profiles or drawings, is finally carried out. In this process, the coloring material is intimately linked to the fabric.

In the final process of bringing the designs to the fabric, there are often several different techniques that come together to ensure that the result is true to what the designer intended.

For example, you may find the same garment, but with different effects and techniques of screenprinting applied, and exhibiting the work of industrial or hand embroidery.

The use of multiple techniques is possible by technological advances that constantly generate new possibilities for the printing and embroidery, offering a wide range of methods with which to manipulate the fabric.

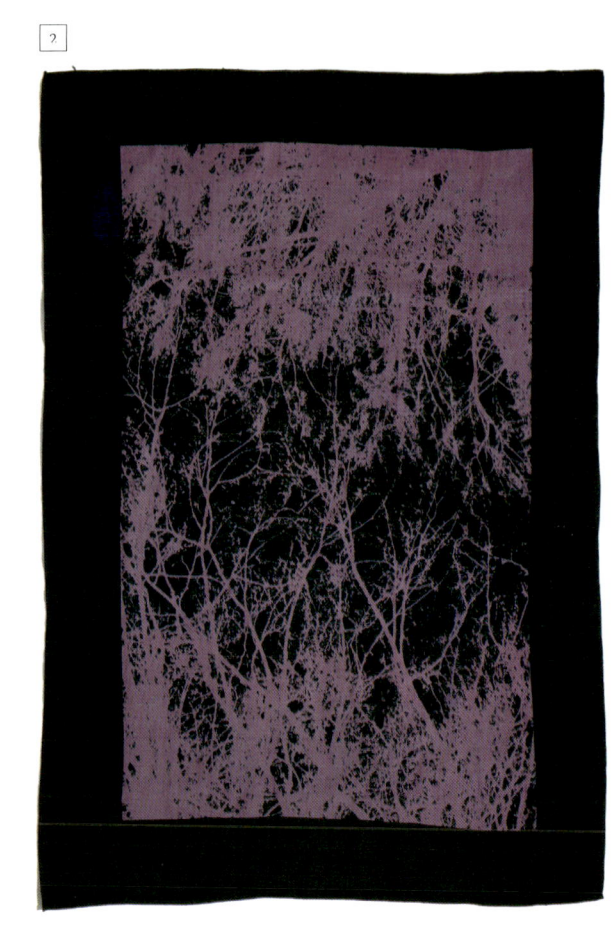

1

2

98 APPLYING THE DESIGNS TO FABRIC: the final result

1. Screenprinting in a single color on red silk. By Javier Nanclares.

2. Printing a single-color ink, pink, on green silk.

3. Fabric decorated with a combination of screenprinting and industrial embroidery, with threads of various colors and sequins.

4. Printed paper for which one needs ten silk-screens to achieve that same number of colors. From the Lissa Italia company.

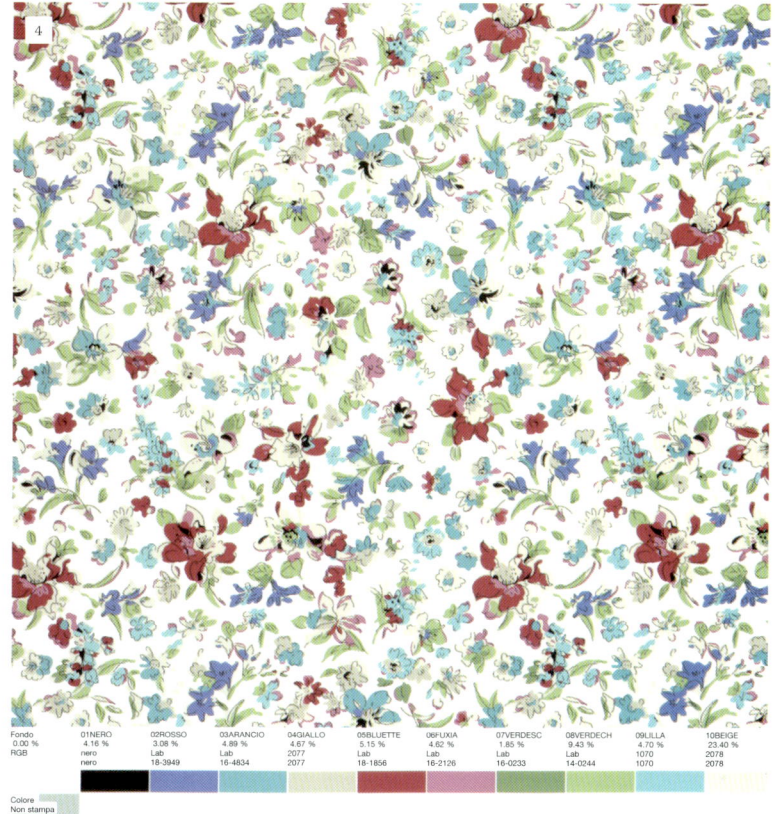

final printing processes 99

SCREENPRINTING

One frequently used printing technique is screenprinting, or serigraphy. This consists of separating the drawing to be transferred to the fabric into different layers that correspond to each of the colors contained in the design. For each of these layers, there is a stencil with the picture you want to appear on the black, opaque screen. Then, the design is placed on arectangular frame of wood or metal, which holds the screen, a special, taut fabric, to which emulsion has already been applied. The light fixes the emulsion and leaves free the mesh areas that will need to be inked. After removing the screen, it is washed to remove the emulsion in areas where the picture appears. The emulsion will cover the areas where there will be no image, leaving free the area in which you want to print the color.

This process is repeated using a screen for each color to be printed. The design is transferred to the fabric by pressing the ink through each screen and onto the fabric underneath. When screenprinting is done manually, a person runs the press and pushes the squeegee to press the ink onto the fabric underneath. In a similar manner, when the process is done industrially, the fabric moves along a conveyor belt and the screens in each part of the design are placed on the fabric, and a mechanical arm spreads the ink over the screen.

Another method of screenprinting involves first dyeing the fabric, and then printing the picture with a corrosive paste that will remove the color. Generally, the is done on dark backgrounds.

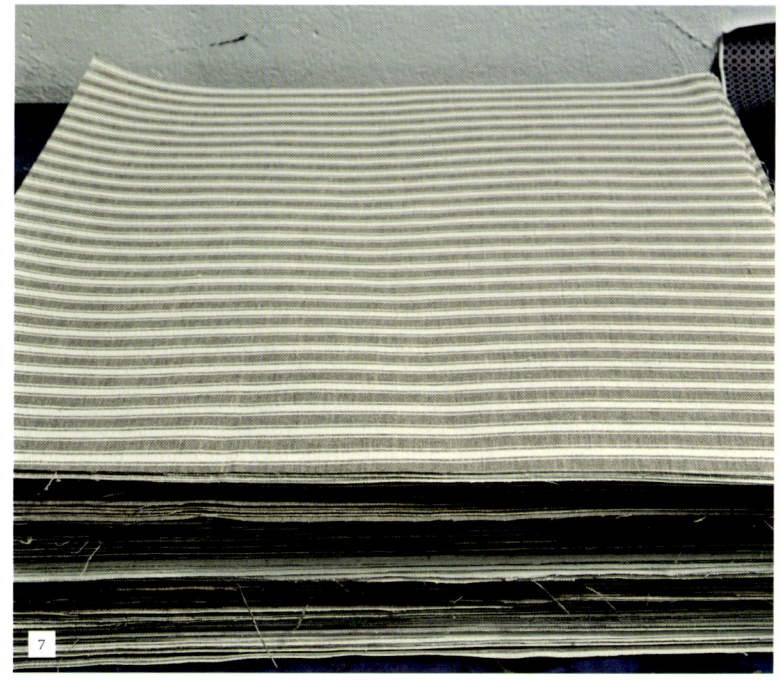

Different stages of industrial screenprinting in a specialized workshop.

4. Screen with a design of simple lines.

5. Industrial process machine with several screens that requires a person to place and remove the fabric. The screen must be larger than the fabric in order to perform a complete printing.

6. The machine lowers the screen onto the fabric, applying emulsion while using a spatula to distribute the color.

7. Stacked, printed fabrics.

1. Silk-screen for the color blue. It works as a negative image. The screen with the drawing will appear as black opaque so that no light reaches the screen.

2. The rearview of a completed screen ready to be printed for a single color. When the color is applied with a squeegee on the screen, the pigment penetrates through the screen, marking the drawing on the fabric underneath.

3. Sample of a black background printed with five colors: yellow, white, green, red, and blue. The dark background has required the use of opaque plastisols in order to obtain the vivid and bright colors. These, in turn, are sensitive to the touch, because they generate a thick covering of paint.

final printing processes **101**

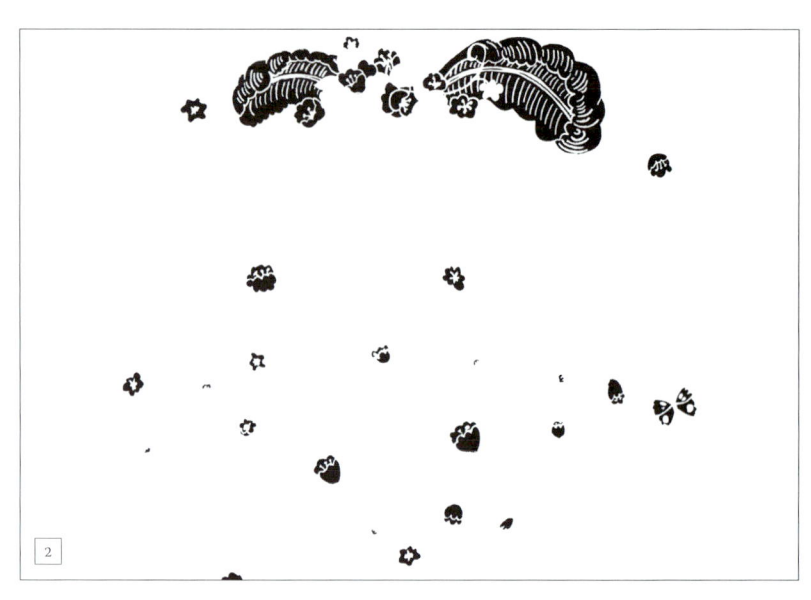

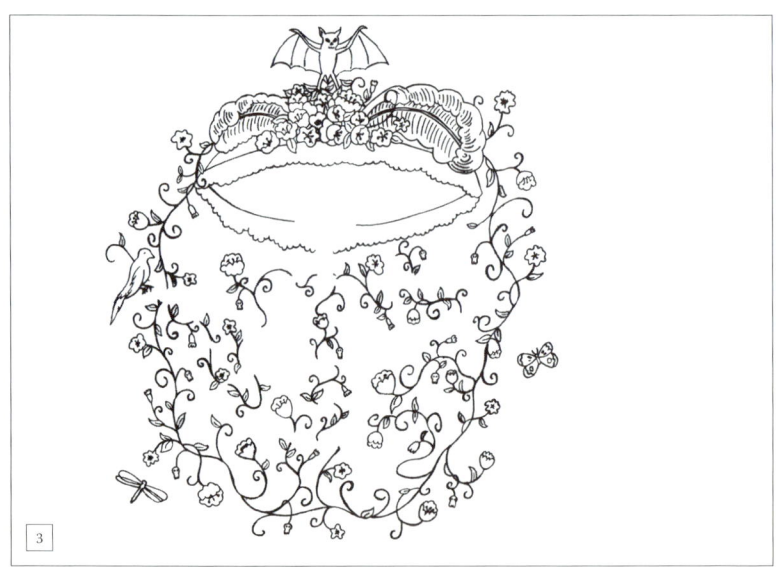

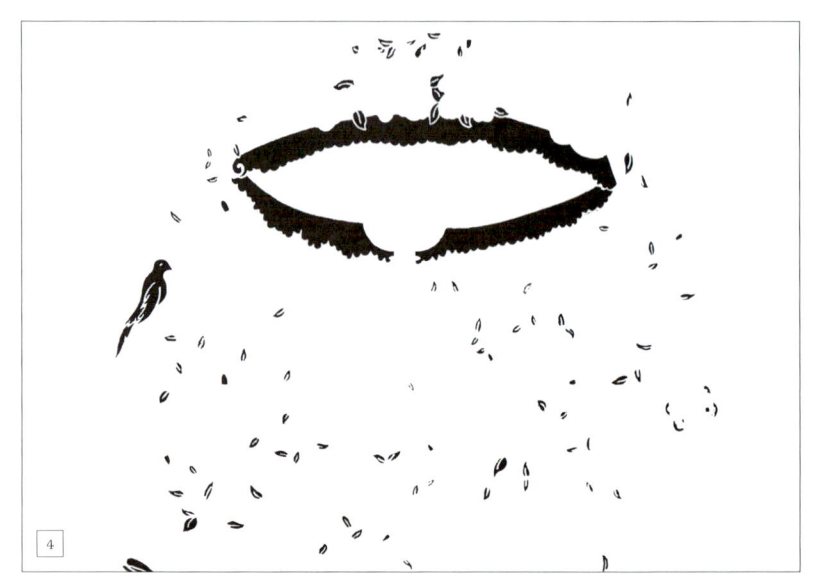

102 APPLYING THE DESIGNS TO FABRIC: the final result

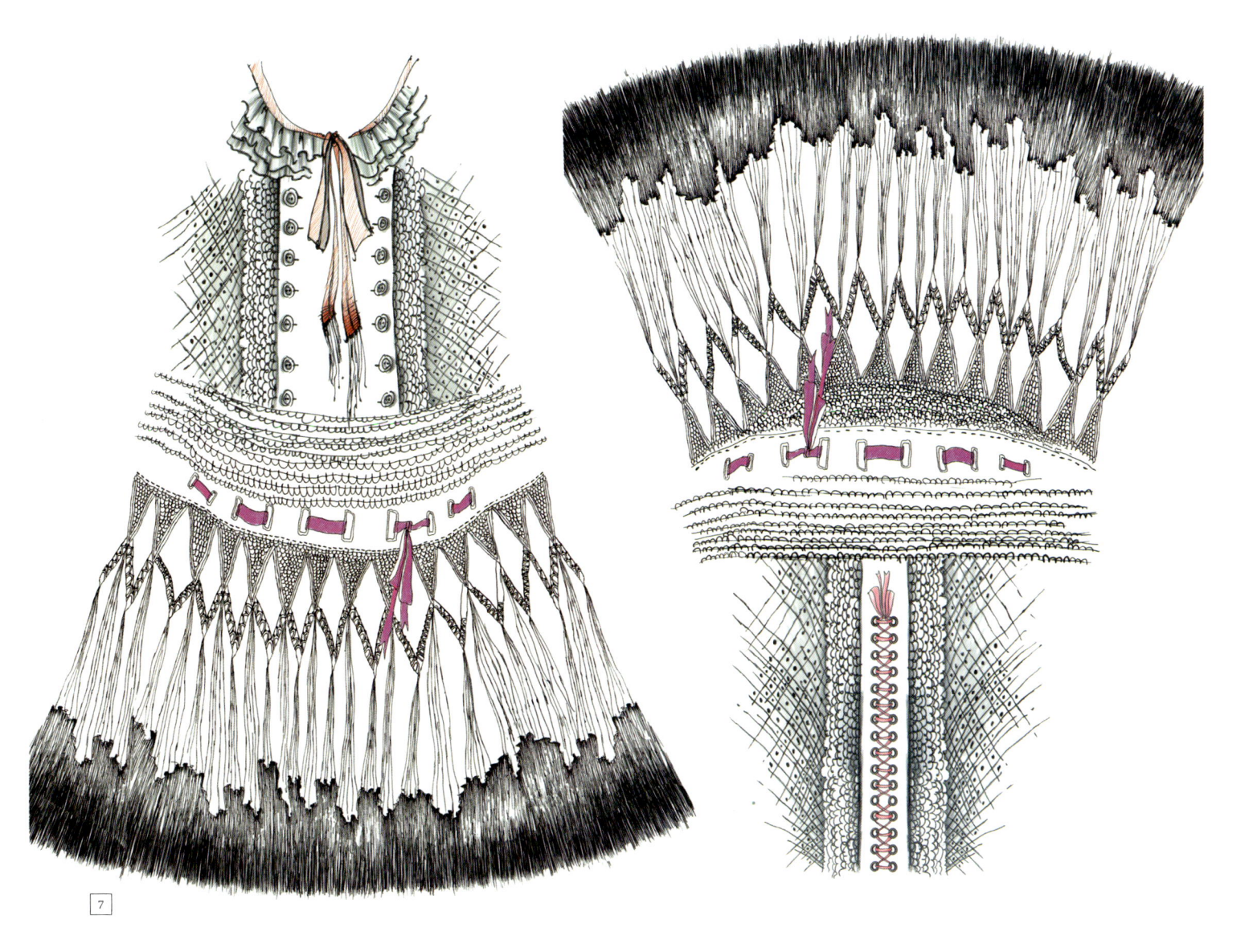

1-2-3-4. Screens for each of the four colors in the drawing.

5. Positional design of four colors on black background. From the Mátala Mamá company.

6. The design applied on a dress. From the Mátala Mamá company.

7-8. The design on this garment takes up the entire surface, taking into account that the ribbon is positional. The result of the screenprinting on the garment is shown on page 49. From the Miriam Ocáriz company.

final printing processes 103

DEVORÉ

The relief effect known as devoré is also obtained through a screenprinting process when printing with known chemicals, like devoré paste, on a fabric with fibers from different groups. Devoré paste is an ink that, by definition, destroys cotton. For example, in a garment with a blend of cotton and polyester, the cotton becomes detached in the area that had been previously printed, and the polyester remains, creating a relief effect. If the portion of cotton that comprises the fabric is greater than that of polyester, the effect is more noticeable.

1. Printed with devoré effect, a result of the subtraction of the velvet cotton in specific areas, which leaves evidence of a polyester base.

2. Drawing prepared for sending to the workshop where the printing will be carried out, which will result in the devoré.

3. Design for carrying out a false devoré on women's T-shirts through printing with the tail and transferring to velvet. By Laura Fernandez.

Color 1 ground
Col. 210 milky petrol

Color 2 softhand print
Col. 269 inky green

Color 3 softhand print
Col. 209 teal green

• Crystals

the final printing process **105**

DIGITAL PRINTING

Digital printing (offset and inkjet) is the great technological advancement in recent years, as far as reproducing images. It is carried out with a large printer that has been prepared to transfer a design to a great variety of surfaces—among them, the fabric. With this device, it is possible to print any type of image, from the most complex of drawings to photographs, without limiting colors or effects. For this to happen, the designer must present the motif to be printed in a digital format, preferably with the extensions .tiff or .eps. The result is of a definition and accuracy that gives the designer great creative freedom. Thanks to this process, stencils, screens, and other usually indispensable equipment becomes unnecessary.

Another of its great advantages is that it produces samples with great speed and facilitates the control of the process through immediate corrections, without wasting time or money. Digital printing does not waste ink, and that's why it's a clean and ecological method to use. This technique is constantly evolving, so the industry annually organizes fairs in different cities around the world, where it displays the latest technology and new possibilities for printing. These are unmissable events for everyone who needs to be up to date on the latest innovations and who wants to take advantage of them the most.

1. Silk gauze printed digitally. From the Lissa Italia company.

2-3-4-5. Photographic effects digitally printed on this collection of silk handkerchiefs. By Javier Nanclares.

the final printing process **107**

	01VIOLASC	01VIOLACH	03FUXIA	04ARANCIO	05GIALLO	06TURCHESESC	07TURCHESECH	08OCRASC	09OCRACH	10BEIGE
	3.62 %	6.21 %	2.37 %	4.52 %	10.28 %	2.49 %	3.63 %	9.56 %	7.57 %	5.95 %
	2042	2043	2044	1850	322	158	666	976	1723	669
	2042	2043	2044	1850	322	158	666	976	1723	669

Colore	12Fondo
Non stampa	27.93 %
	1114
	1114

108 APPLICATION OF THE DESIGNS TO FABRIC: the final result

Digitally printed paper with a variety of colors. From the Lissa Italia company.

the final printing process **109**

EMBROIDERY

Embroidery is a needlework technique by which designs can be produced on textile fabrics. Its application aims to both decorate the fabric and reproduce a design. Embroidery appears on top of the material. Knitted fabrics are also often incorporated in their construction in embellishments, such as pearls, woven glasses, sequins, gems, tapes, and ribbons. Textile manufacturers use this technique to produce fabrics that often turn out to be exquisite works of craftsmanship. In some cases, they highlight the properties of the fabric through brightness and textures, and in others, they manipulate the fabric to make exciting surface shapes and forms. An example of this is the work of the British designer Anne Kyrö Quinn (see p. 184), who builds here textiles through height and textures, with an almost architectural vision.

TYPES OF EMBROIDERY

HEMSTITCH. Traditional trimming technique in which threads are pulled together in a group, creating a series of tiny, bead-like openings, and a hem.
CROSS-STITCH. A basic technique that consists of forming crosses by pulling a few threads through a fabric.
PALESTRINA STITCH. Also known as the Old English knot stitch. Rows of knots are placed together to form a textured surface.
CHAIN STITCH. This stitch resembles a crochet chain and its function is essentially the same.
PARMA EMBROIDERY. Consists of a four-sided pattern, in same-color threads on a cheaply woven fabric.
LAGARTERA EMBROIDERY. Type of elaborate Spanish embroidery that uses satin and double running stitches. There are two main variants: open (sunk) and closed.
HARDANGER. Very difficult, but exquisite, Norwegian embroidery. It is stitched white on white and contains solid blocks of stitches contrasting with lacy open work.
ENHANCEMENT. Embroidery used to enhance designs or to provide eye-catching initials and logos.
RICHELIÉU EMBROIDERY. Consists in cutting away the fabric and working over the edges with stitches, such as the buttonhole stitch.
EMBROIDERY ON TULLE. Small, decorative elements mechanically applied to tulle.
SMOCKING. An embroidery stitch that is traditionally used on children's clothes. It produces a honeycomb-looking effect.
MANILA EMBROIDERY. The origin of this embroidery lies in China. Very well-known for its application on typical hand-embroidered Spanish shawls called "Manila shawls." It is also applied to other items, such as kimonos, cushions, and tables. Traditionally, they were done in silk and embroidered by hand with nature motifs and other characteristic Chinese designs.

An alternative to handmade embroidery is the industrial option, which is done by machine. An example of this is the transfer of sequins, glass, and applications with special effects, which are placed on the fabric by thermobonding. The great advantage of industrial embroidery is the large number of garments that can be embroidered in a comparatively short amount of time. However, it does lack the creative quality that a craftsperson, who likes working with her hands and experimenting with stitches, could produce.

1. Prototype design by María José Lleonar for the Simorra company.

2. Hand embroidery with cotton threads of various colors, with applications of stones. From the Ventures India company.

3-4-5-6. Drawings and industrial prototypes with embroidery, for enhancement **(4)**, and in Manila **(6)**. By María José Lleonar from the Simorra company.

7-8. Specification sheets for embroidery to be done in an industrial embroidery workshop.

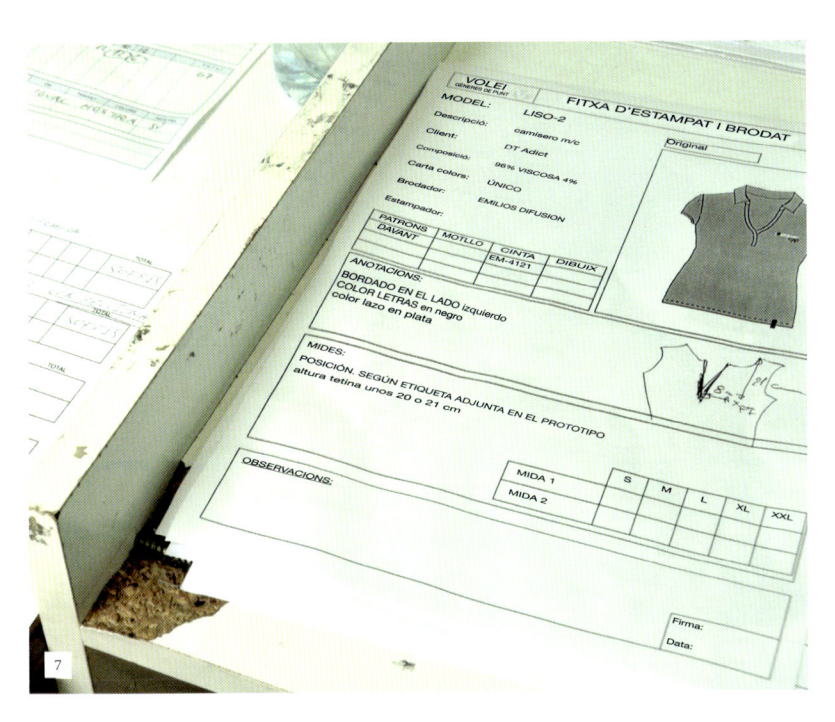

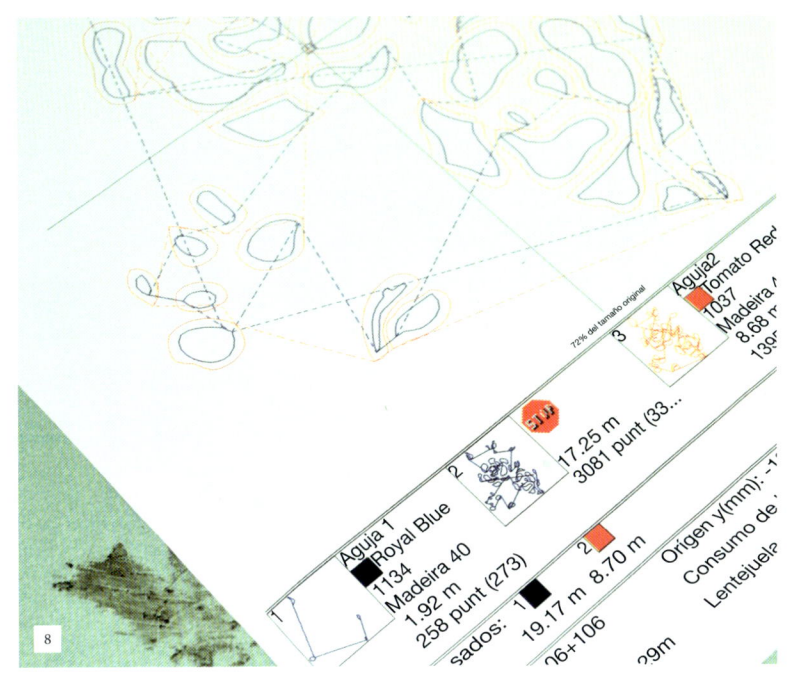

the final printing process **111**

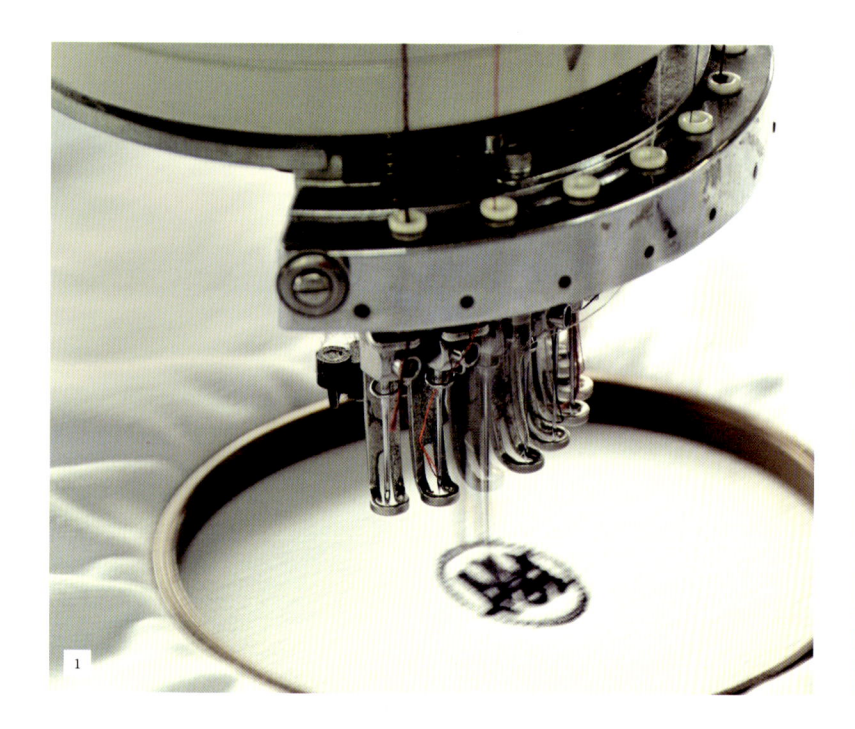

112 APPLICATION OF THE DESIGNS TO FABRIC: the final result

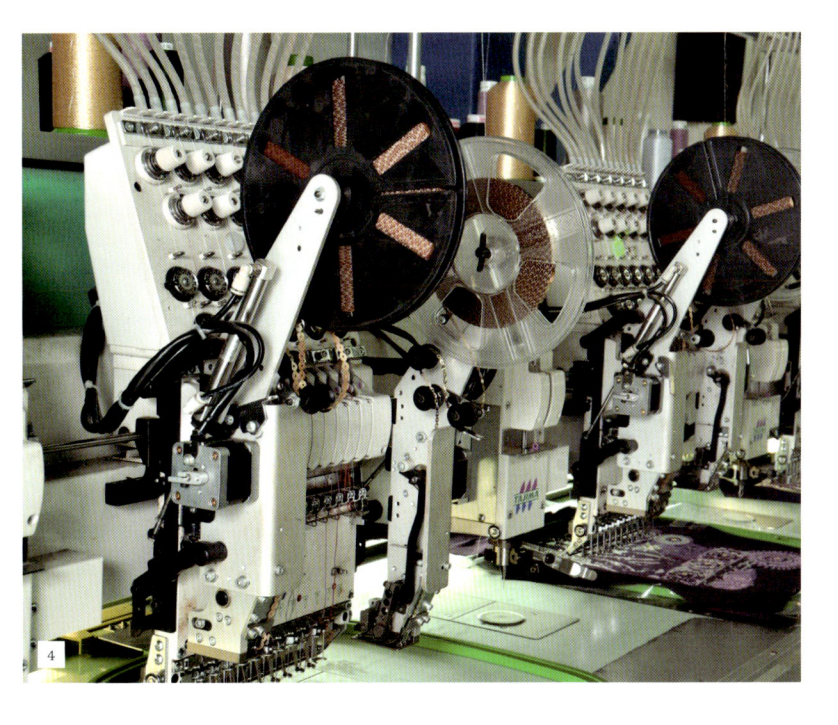

1-2. Industrial embroidery workshop in which embroidery is worked onto a frame.

3. Industrial embroidery. From the Cadena company.

4. Industrial machinery for application of embroidery and sequins.

5. Sample of fabric with embroidery and sequins, after the printing process.

6. Machine that carries out transfers with applications.

7. Prototype of industrial chain stitch embroidery that combines two colors and two fabrics.

8. Transfers to be applied to the fabric by thermobonding.

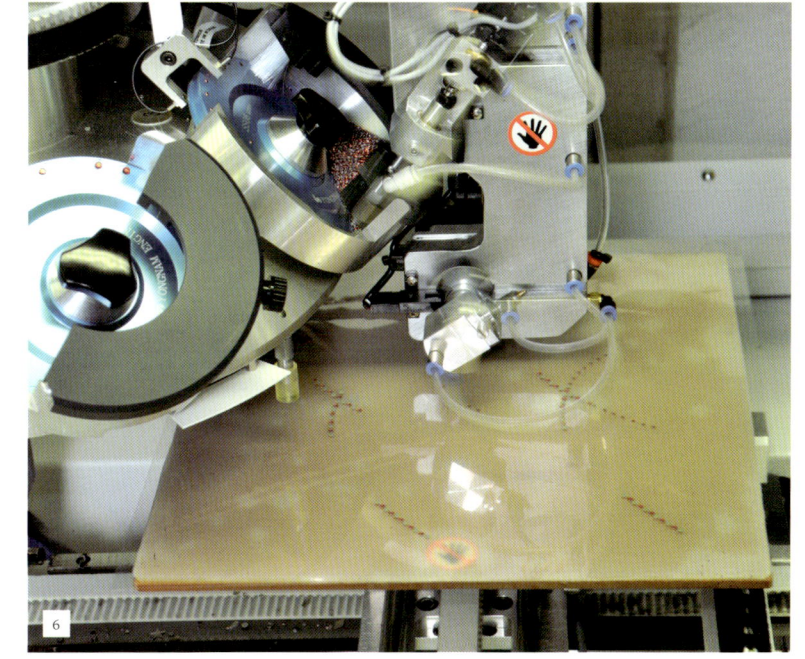

the final printing process 113

Haute couture allows embroiderers to present exquisite designs without sacrificing creativity or accruing great costs. From the Christian Dior company. Haute couture collection Winter 2008.

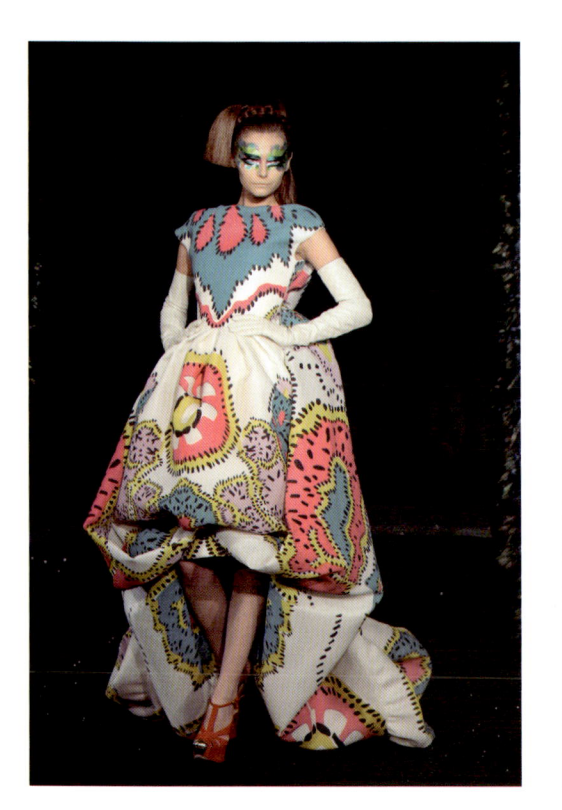

114 APPLICATION OF THE DESIGNS TO FABRIC: the final result

Hand embroidery carried out in India, with silk, silver, and gold threads, and applications of sequins and stones on a base of silk fabric for undergarments. By Manuel Albarrán.

the final printing process **115**

MATERIAL FOR EMBROIDERING

Threads used in embroidery vary greatly in quality, thickness, and texture. They also come in a wide range of colors. Ornaments and applique can also be used in the embroidery. The threads that are used in this technique are the same ones that are used for the woven fabric, but the most common are the classics cotton, silk, polyester, wool, and linen, and even silver and gold threads are used in the different media included in the art of stitching.

Likewise, there are combinations that generate new effects, such as the twist, composed of three twisted threads; the wavy thread, which can be done in gold or silver; using a thread of greater thickness; using a thread with lateral notches; and finally, there is one combination that can be presented as curly, smooth, matte, or shiny, in several degrees of thickness.

The most frequently seen ornaments are pearls, glass and crystal by Swarovski, sequins of several sizes, and chained, precious or imitation stones, fabrics, ribbons, and tapes.

1-2-3-4-5. Embroideries with different threads of silk taffeta. From the Ventures India company.

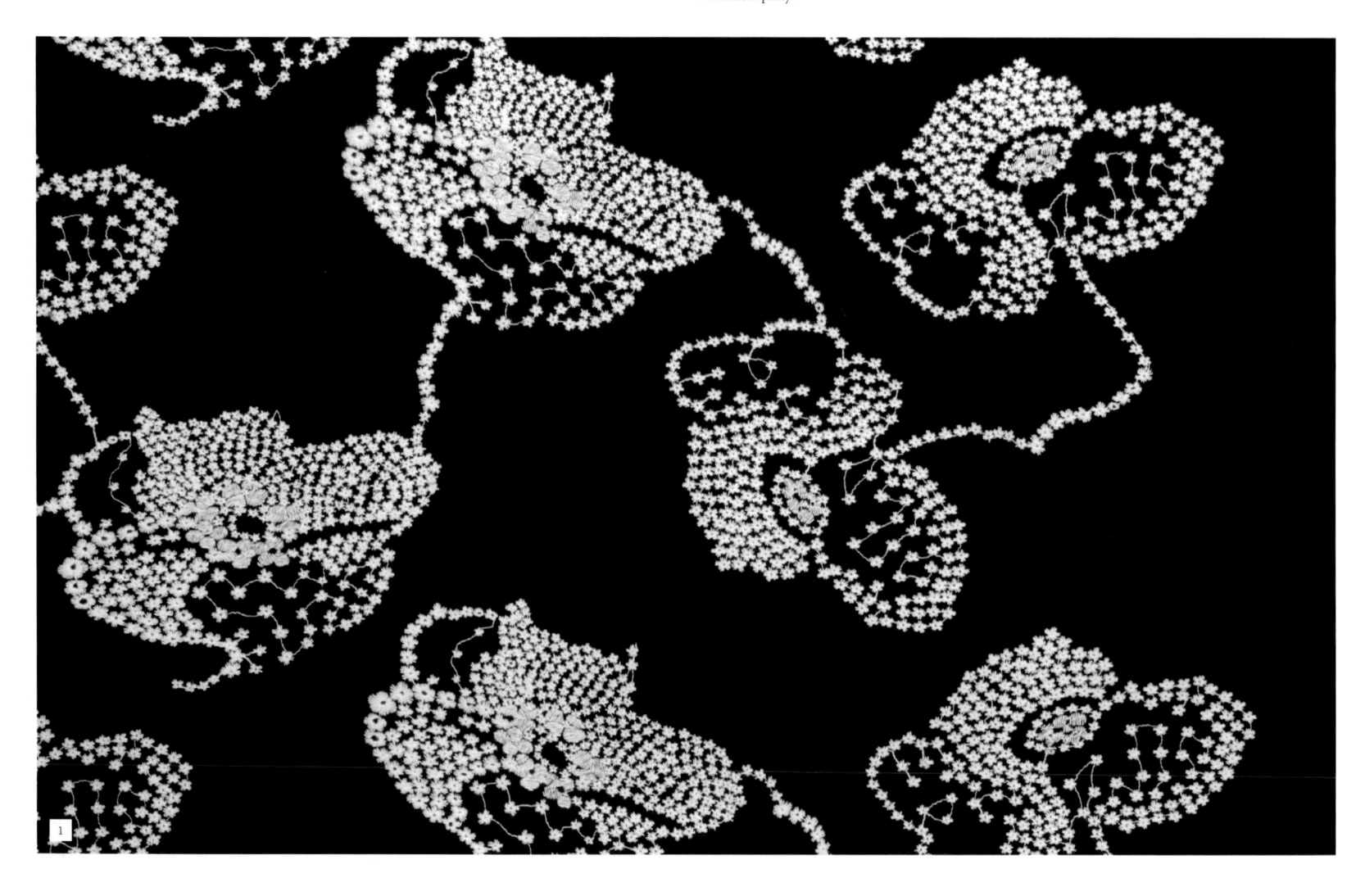

116 APPLICATION OF THE DESIGNS TO FABRIC: the final result

the final printing process **117**

ROLLER PRINTING

This system was developed in the period when textile operations were first mechanized (from 1785). The technique consists of a cylinder or roller of cast iron and another of copper engraved with the design, under which slides the fabric that is to be printed with successive applications of color. These cylinders turn to a container, from where they take up the color. Because the cylinders are quite costly, and because each can print only one color, this system is almost never used today.

THERMOTRANSFERENCE OR SUBLIMATION

Printing through thermotransference is a procedure in which the designs are transferred to the fabric with heat and pressure through a paper specially printed by rotogravure, offset, or screenprinting.

The fabric or garment is placed on a plastic frame and dampened in a special solution. The paper with the design is placed on the fabric, which remains taut on a frame, then moistened in a special solution, and covered with a layer of silicon-treated oilskin.

The set is treated with pressure and heat until the drawing is vaporized and the design is passed to the fabric. Through this method, one obtains better penetration of the dye in the fabric, greater compatibility between design and printing, smaller industrial costs, and less pollution. Nowadays, this process is also carried out digitally.

1. Printing through thermotransference.

2. Design of complex composition, suitable to be carried out industrially, with a system of rollers for a four-color printing process. From the Basso & Brooke company.

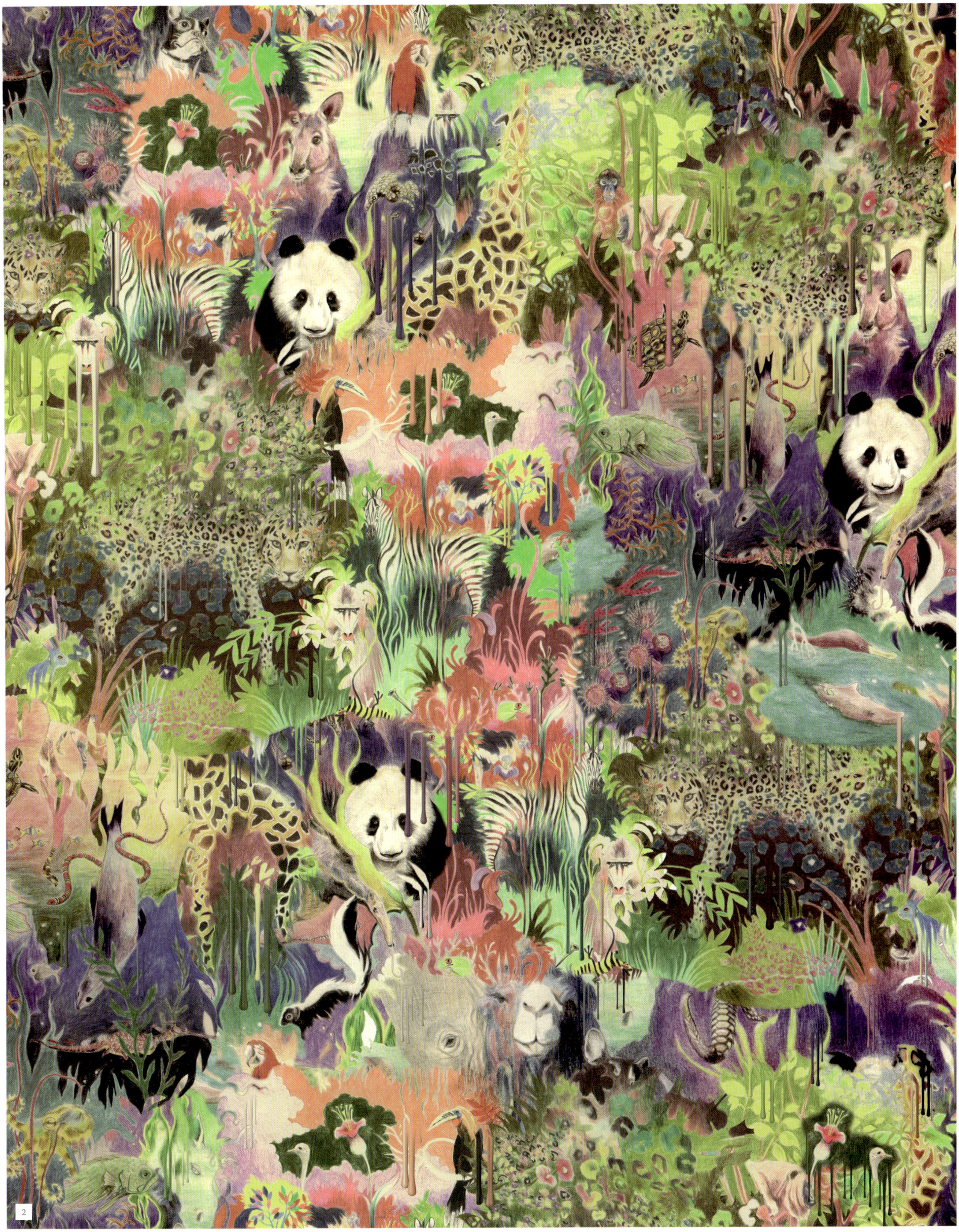
2

1. Traditional Indian blocks used for printing on textiles.
2. Linoleum blocks and materials used for printing.
3. Design printed with linoleum blocks.

BLOCK PRINTING

Printing with stamp pads is one of the oldest techniques. It consists of carving the surface of a hard material (such as wood, linoleum, or rubber) to obtain an image in negative relief. The resulting stamp pad, or block, is then inked and pressure is applied, which leaves the designed image on the fabric. In 1834, printing with blocks became mechanized. The technique allowed their mass production with a variety of motifs and colors.

Traditionally, blocks for printing have been made of wood, although, especially in Europe, a great number were made of metal attached to a wood base. The woods most suitable for the making of blocks are those that have a dense grain, the hard and resistant kind, such as box, beech, or sycamore, among others.

The making of blocks, or wooden stamps, requires a very specialized aptitude, for which the skill of wood carving is most important. Woodcutting is a complex discipline that requires not only skill in handling tools, but also a knowledge of wood grains and cross grains. The making of these blocks is a discipline that traditionally has been done by master craftsmen and is not practiced much at present.

120 APPLICATION OF THE DESIGNS TO FABRIC: the final result

the final printing process **121**

RESIST PRINTING

In these prints, the drawing is defined when one dyes a previously treated fabric so that the color does not penetrate specific areas; this is usually called "resist printing." Batik is a well-known and simple version of this technique. In this case, the design is drawn with hot wax, so that, when it solidifies, it works as an insulating layer. Therefore, when the fabric is dyed, the covered areas remain reserved, or unprinted. The colors are worked from light to dark, while covering new parts with wax and dyeing the design again until it is completed. At the end of the process, the wax is removed with a solvent or with heat.

Another common technique is *shibori*, a Japanese term that is applied generically to variously used procedures for dyeing fabrics using resists. Unlike with batik, areas are not covered with wax, but through procedures of bundling, sewing, bending, rolling up, and gathering.

One of the most attractive features of this technique is that it implies a certain degree of unpredictability; while keeping within the general desired effect, the results are always different.

The Western adaptation of *shibori* is tie-dye, a technique in which a fabric that has been knotted or tied with threads is dyed.

1. Japanese print done in the resist technique known as shibori.

2. Print done in the batik technique.

3. The tie-dye technique obtains a design by knotting the fabric to form the resist.

4. Japanese tie-dye print that was achieved by placing small seeds in the tied part of the fabric to form the resulting pattern.

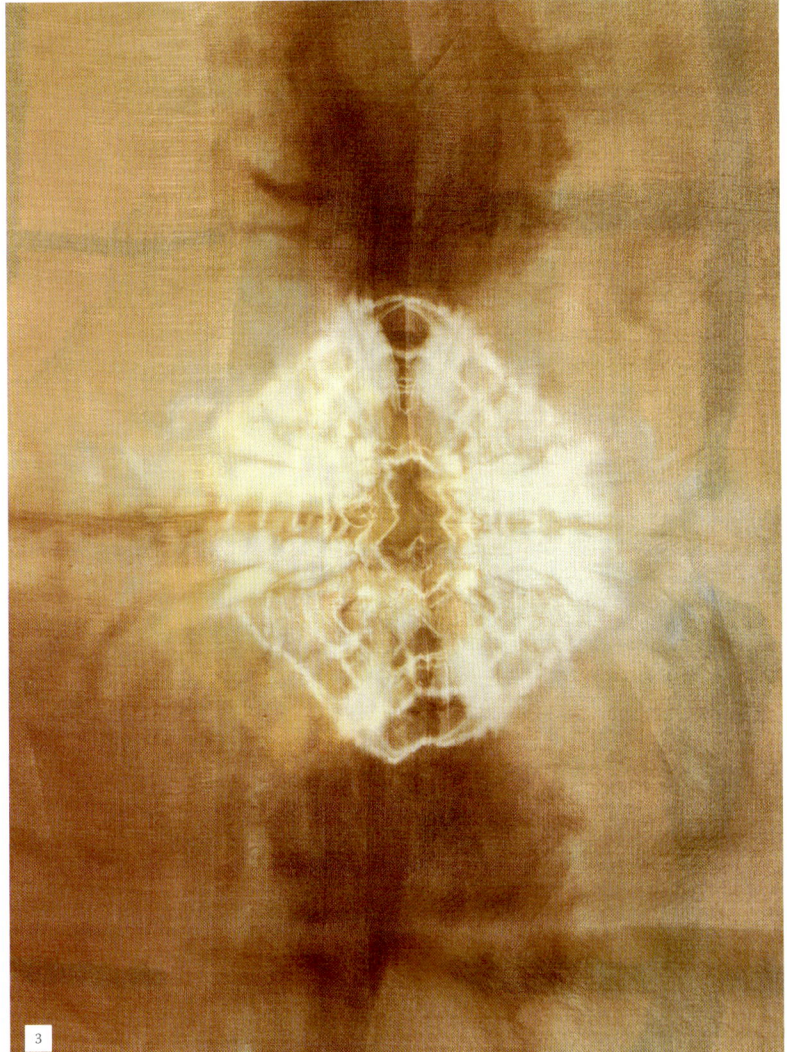

the final printing process **123**

THE FINAL PRODUCT

Fabrics are the most obvious surface on which to print. Frequently, however, textile designers choose to apply prints directly to a specific area of the garment (low collars, pockets, sleeves, or T-shirts), on a handkerchief or scarf, on accessories (bags, belts, socks, gloves, etc.), on applications (patch or ornament), or to the label.

Another factor that must be taken into account when considering the design is the sector of the market to which the garment is directed. The shapes and colors of the motifs will be very different when they are applied to textiles for children, babies, men, or women; clothes for parties, weddings and ceremonies; lingerie and bathing suits or sportswear. The designer has the option of specializing in a specific sector of the market, but the more versatile he or she is, the more employment possibilities will be presented to him or her.

Sometimes, the textile designer and the fashion designer do not have any contact. In these cases, the company or fashion designer will buy the fabric with the already finished design at fairs or through commercial textile companies.

1. This print composed of stains and irregular brushstrokes enhances to the garment's loose feel. From the Sharon Wauchob company.

2. Print that simulates the woven tartan, or Scot, done with a sequential geometrical design of lines and colors and varied proportions. From the Basso & Brooke company.

3. Design composed of threads of different fibers and colors. From the Louis Feraud company.

the final product 125

126 APPLICATION OF THE DESIGNS TO FABRIC: the final result

Inspired by the folklore of the countries of Eastern Europe. By Atelier Lzc for the Adieu Tristesse company.

the final product **127**

128 APPLICATION OF THE DESIGNS TO FABRIC: the final result

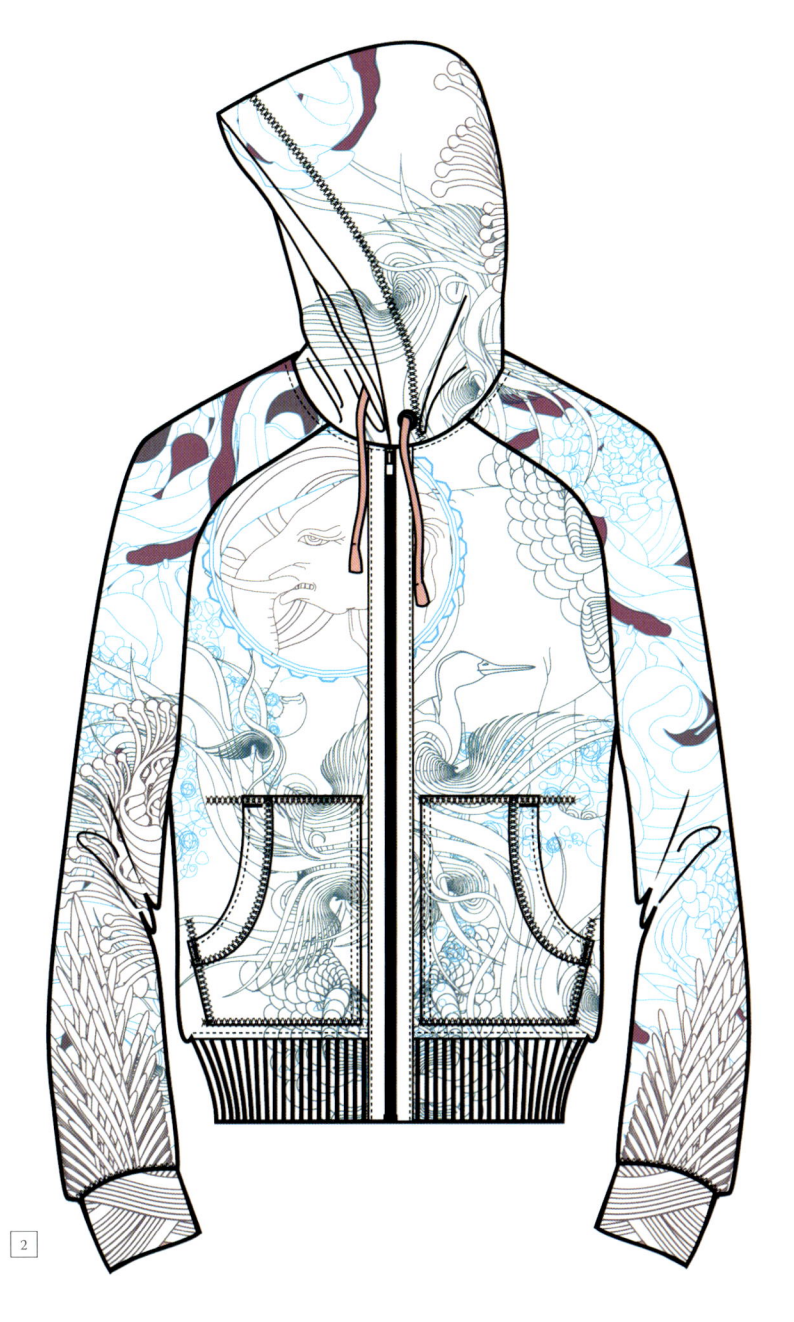

1. Technical drawing of the design entitled "Elephant." From the Artful Dodger company.

2-3. "Elephant" design conceived for embroidery and printing, inspired by Indian iconography and applied to a line of streetwear. By Inocuo The Sign for the Artful Dodger company.

4. "Elephant" design applied on a pullover. From the Artful Dodger company.

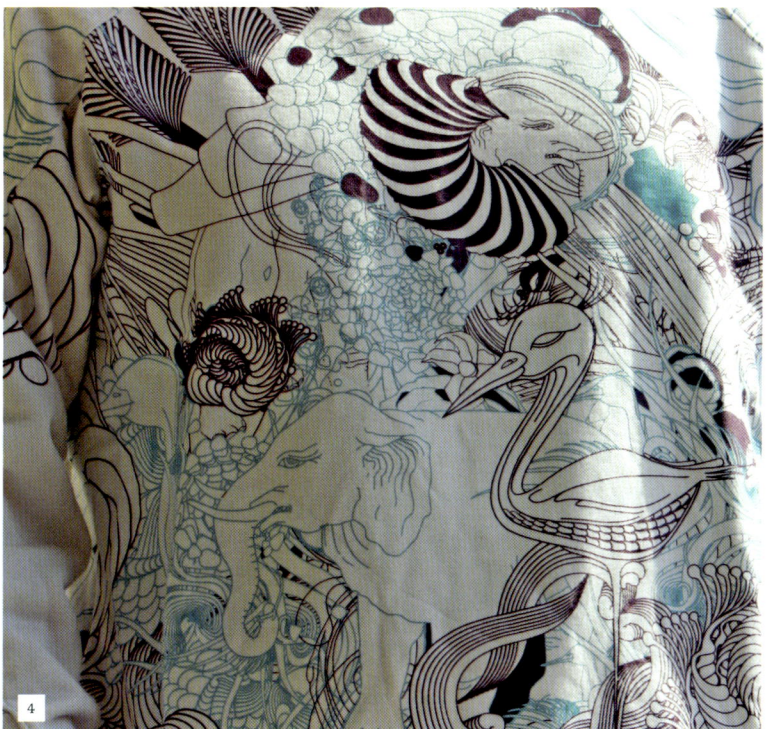

the final product **129**

STYLES AND MOTIFS
gallery

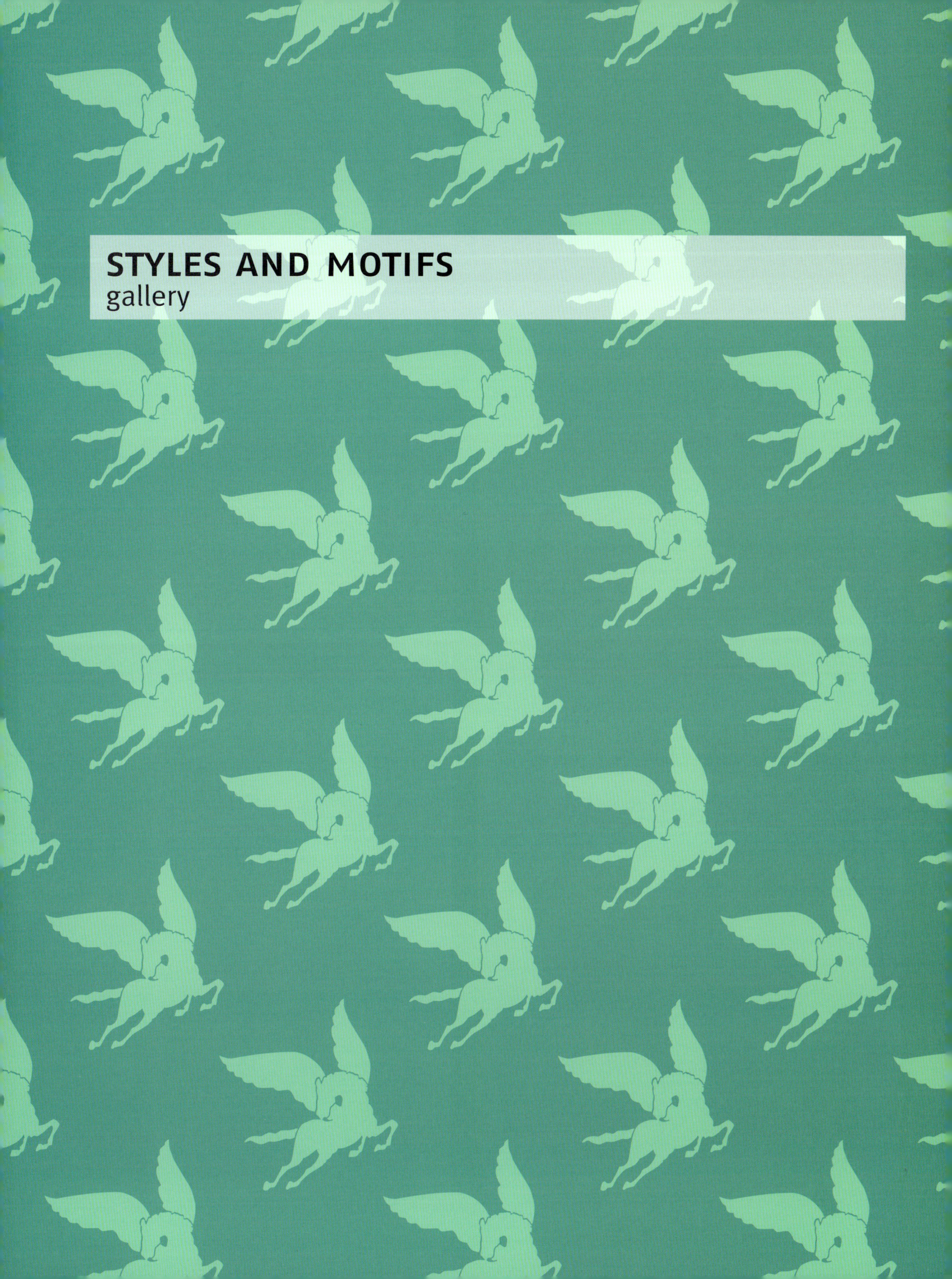

BOTANICAL GARDEN
FLOWERS, FOLIAGE, ROMANTICISM, POP INSPIRATION

Floral and foliage motifs are a source of constant inspiration in fashion, thanks to the infinite aesthetic possibilities they present. Often, the outline and the palette of colors are what define the character of the garment and even of a complete collection. Here, for example, small flowers and soft colors generate a romantic aesthetic, as the exciting forms and psychedelic tones create styles that go from pop-up to ethnic exoticism.

Despite being intimately linked to nature, floral designs give the designer great freedom to create exquisite compositions out of his imagination, which converts every garment into a work of art.

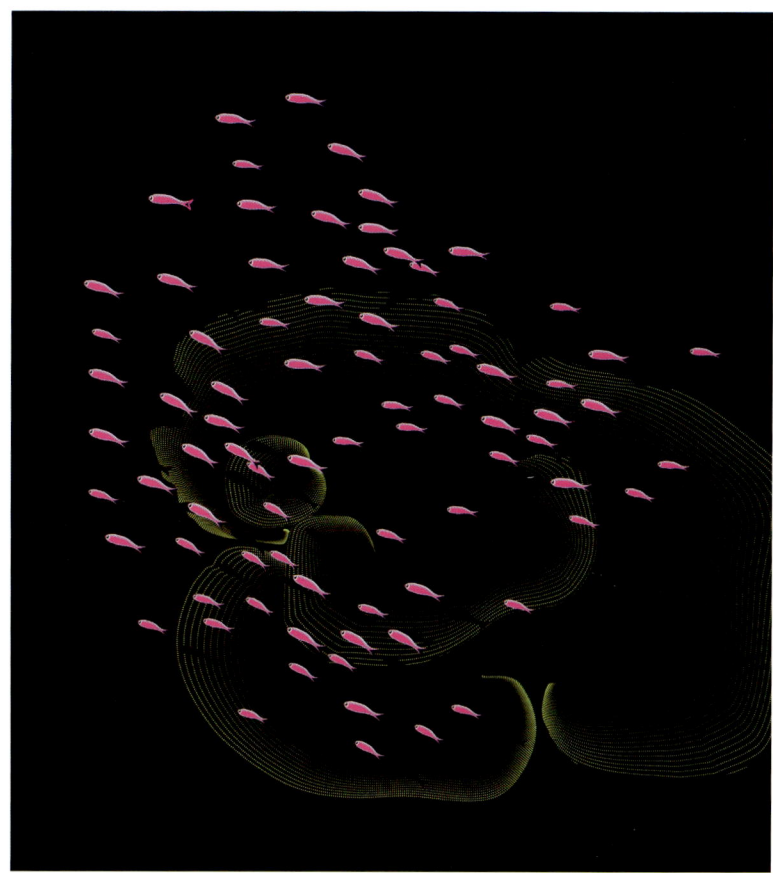

Vectorial images inspired by nature, formed by independent geometrical objects defined by different mathematical attributes of form, position, and color. By Rafa Mollar.

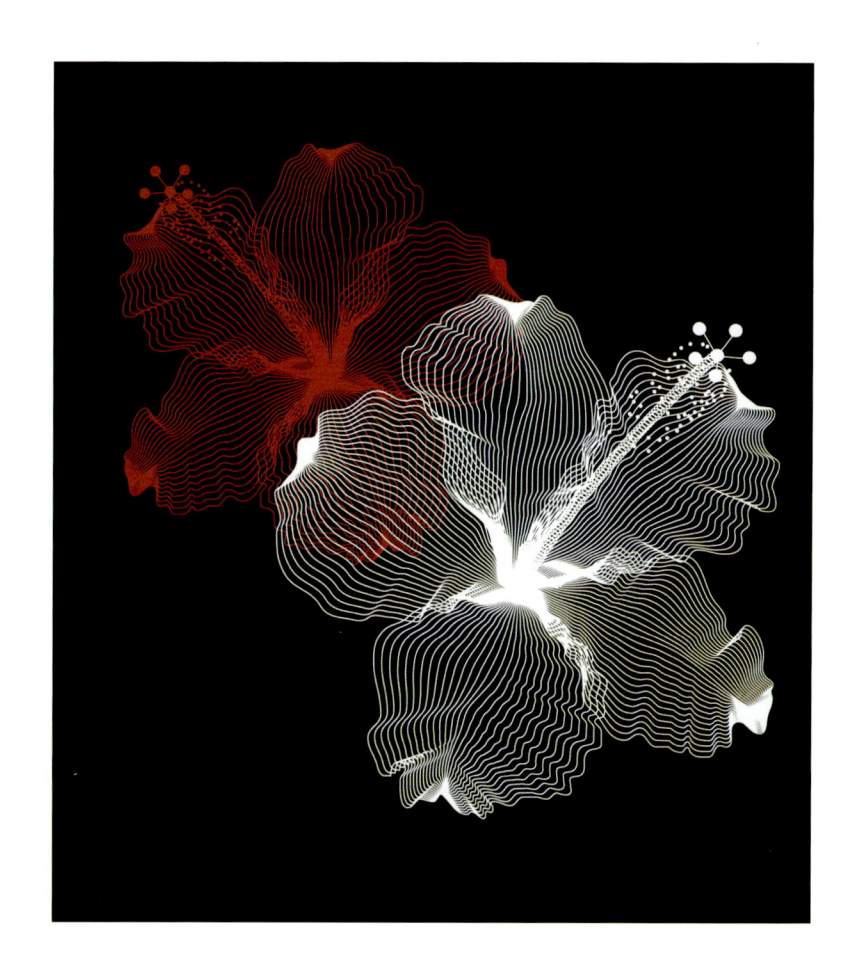

botanical garden **133**

Floral motifs are an inexhaustible source of inspiration. Here, the subject is presented in a wide range of variants, from the abstract to the figurative (WGSN).

botanical garden **135**

136 STYLES AND MOTIFS: gallery

Distinct compositions in which the creative possibilities are appreciated from variations of size and color. From the Sisters Gulassa company.

botanical garden 137

138 STYLES AND MOTIFS: gallery

1. Positional drawing for undergarments. Spring/Summer 2006 collection. By Laura Fernández.

2-3. Designs for continuous prints. Spring/Summer 2006 bath collection. From Oysho.

4-5. Positional drawings from a lingerie collection. Spring/Summer 2006 collection. By Laura Fernández for the Oysho company.

botanical garden **139**

GEOMETRY
LINES AND CIRCLES

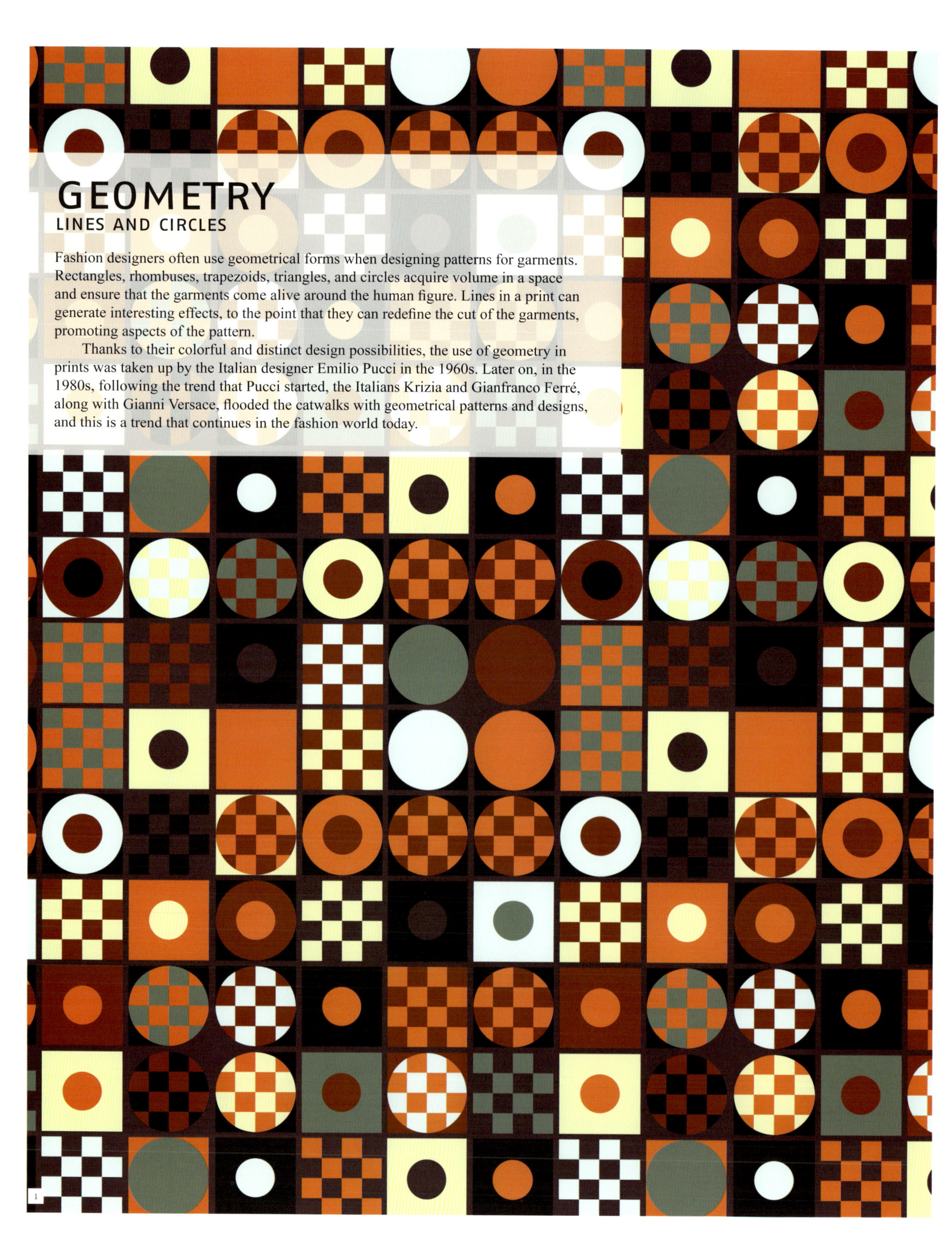

Fashion designers often use geometrical forms when designing patterns for garments. Rectangles, rhombuses, trapezoids, triangles, and circles acquire volume in a space and ensure that the garments come alive around the human figure. Lines in a print can generate interesting effects, to the point that they can redefine the cut of the garments, promoting aspects of the pattern.

Thanks to their colorful and distinct design possibilities, the use of geometry in prints was taken up by the Italian designer Emilio Pucci in the 1960s. Later on, in the 1980s, following the trend that Pucci started, the Italians Krizia and Gianfranco Ferré, along with Gianni Versace, flooded the catwalks with geometrical patterns and designs, and this is a trend that continues in the fashion world today.

1. The digital treatment of the figures gives rise to multiple visual effects (WGSN).

2-3. The composition based on geometric figures generates a print of ethnic style (WGSN).

4. Creation by Hanna Werning for the House of Dagmar company. Spring-Summer 2008 collection.

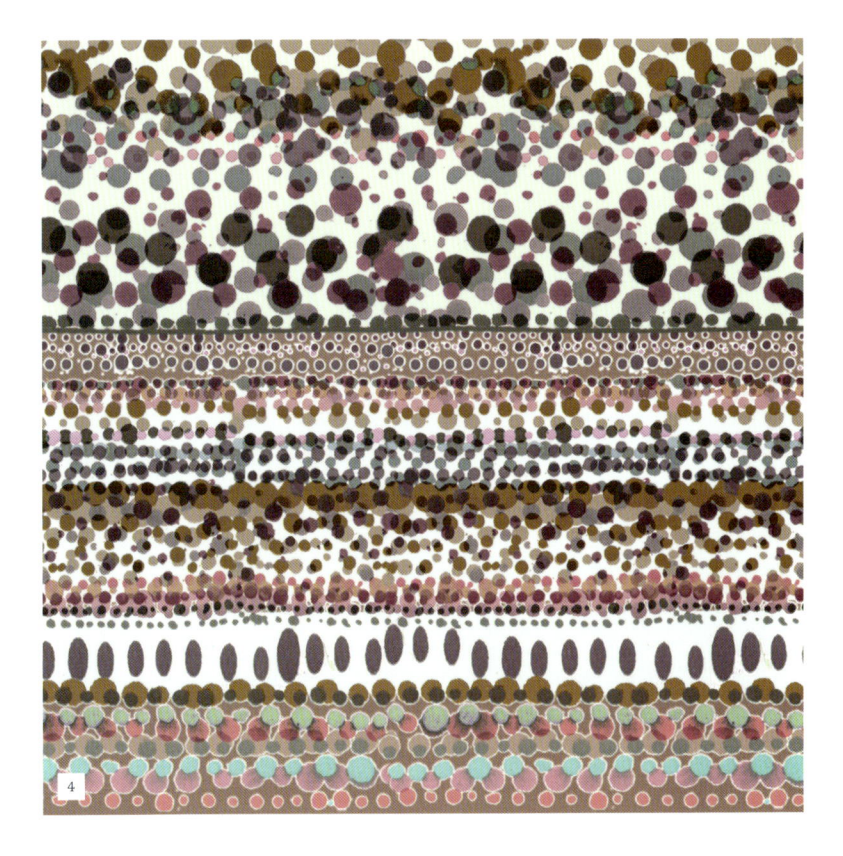

geometry **141**

142 STYLES AND MOTIFS: gallery

New York designer Aimée Wilder takes the inspiration she gleans from contemporary graphic art to her textile designs.

geometry 143

1-2-3-4. Repetition of the same figure with variations in color. By Aimée Wilder.

5-6. Geometrical lines inspired by the Japanese tradition.

144 STYLES AND MOTIFS: gallery

geometry **145**

SPORTY MOTIFS
THE SEA, MOUNTAINS, CITY, COUNTRYSIDE

Outdoor activities and sports have gone from being simple pastimes to a way of life, and fashion, naturally, is inspired by them and keeps up to date with their evolution. From custom images to abstractions, designs on garments often reflect these environments—in these examples, the nautical scene. Indeed, garments frequently reflect the way we look at the world. This has a special relevance at present, when concern for nature and our environment acquire ever greater attention on the catwalks.

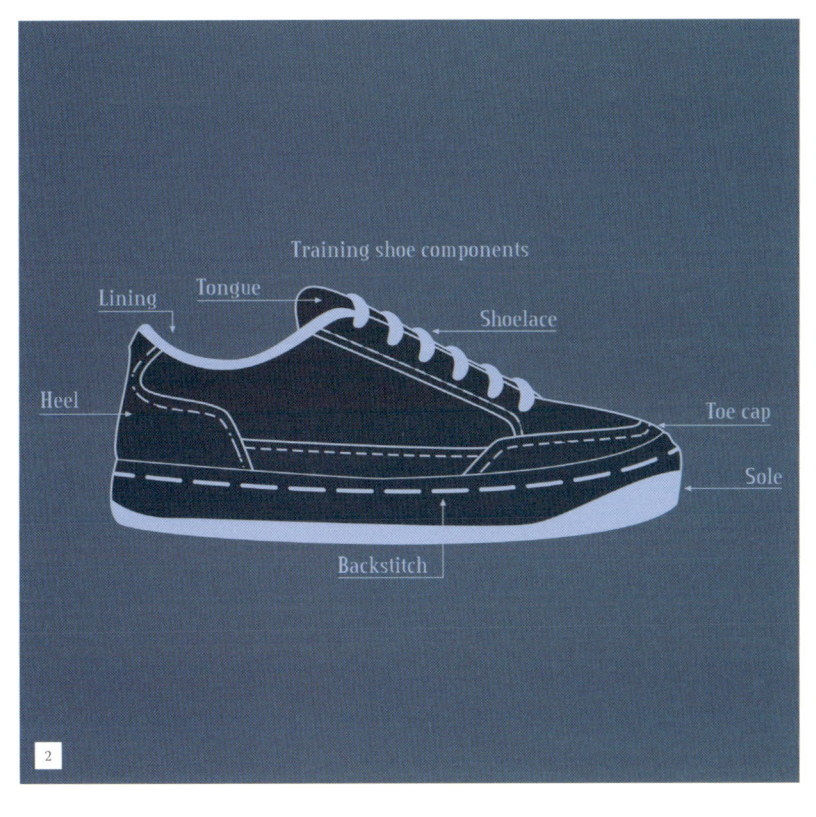

1. Nautical inspirations used for design. By Aimée Wilder.

2-3-4-5. Original drawing and applications on different garments. From the Giulio company.

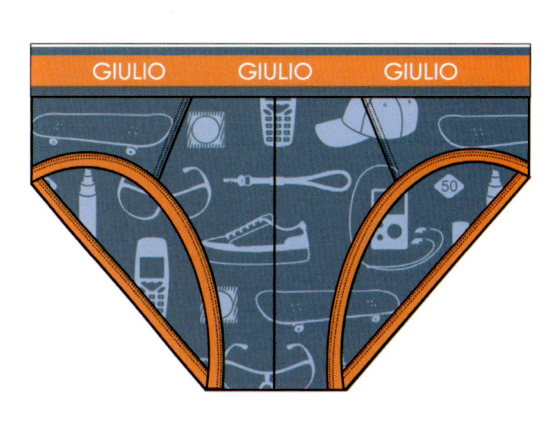

sport life **147**

148 STYLES AND MOTIFS: gallery

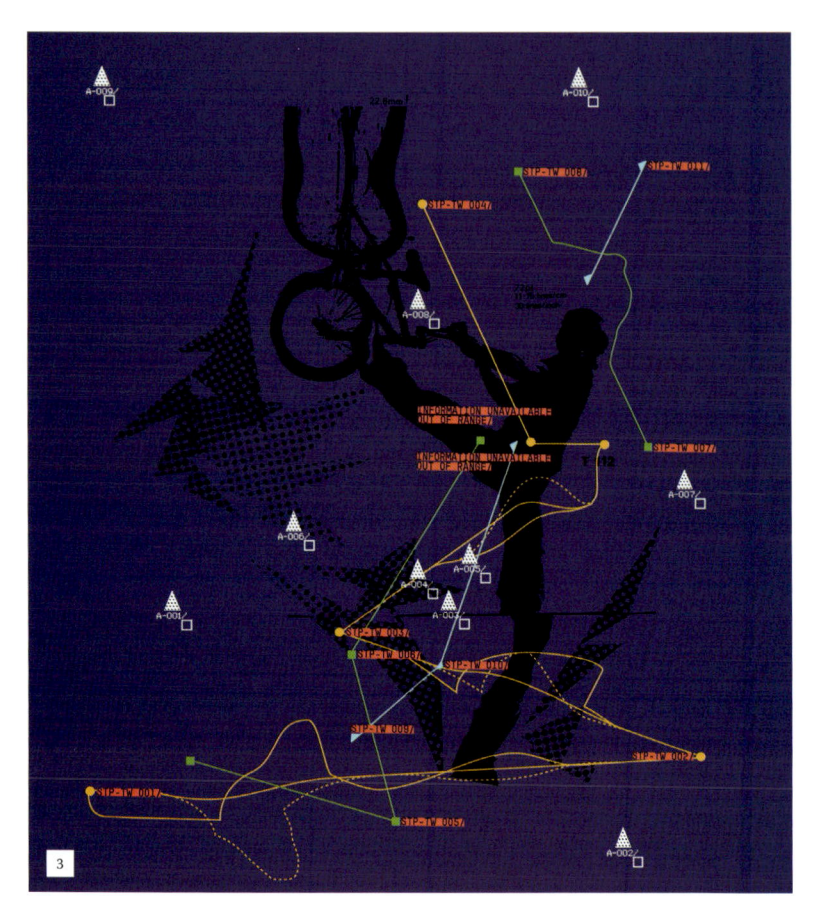

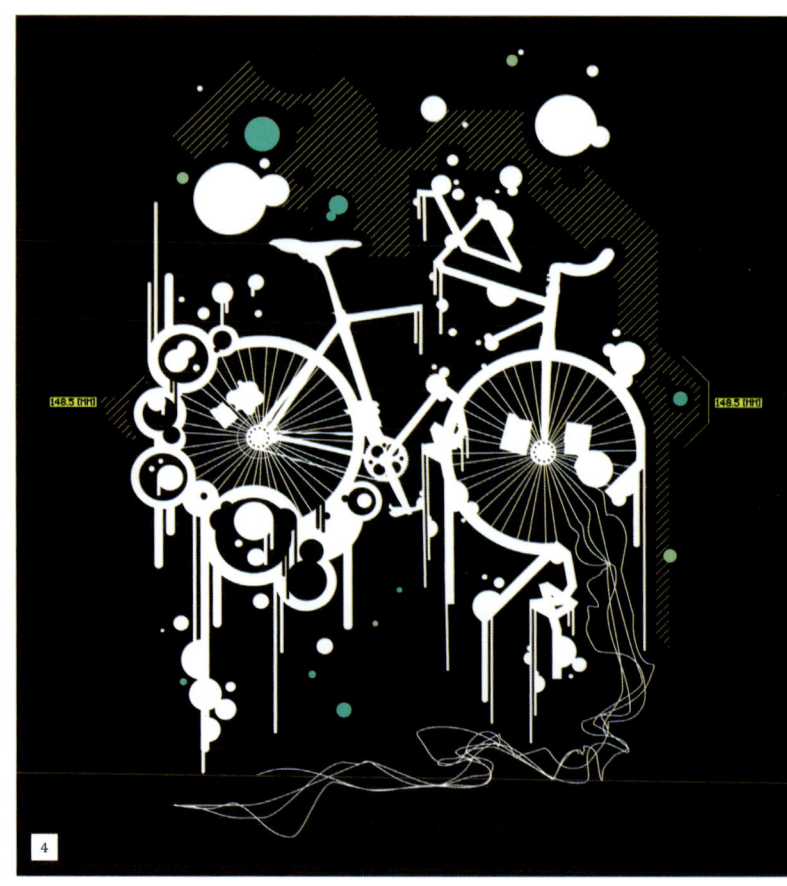

[5]

[6]

1-2-3-4-5. Sport icons prints used for textile patterns (WGSN).

6-7-8. Illustrations for screenprinting on T-shirts (WGSN).

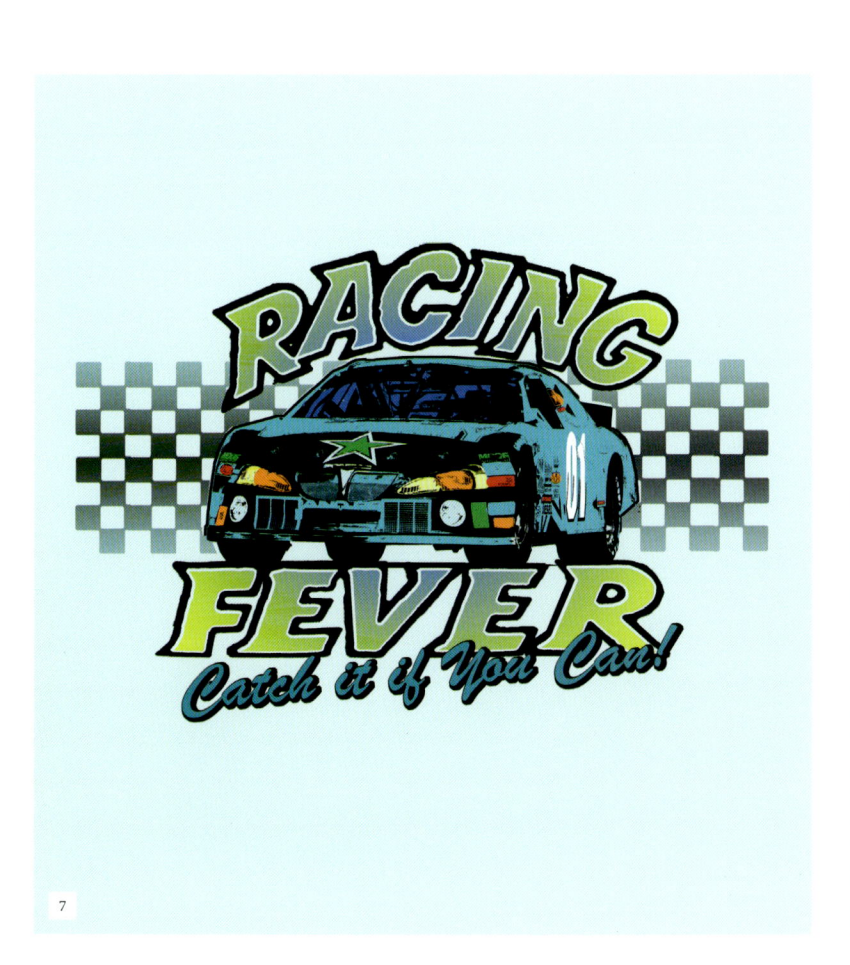

[7]

[8]

sport life **149**

KULTE

THE STANDARD OF EXCELLENCE IN ALL COLOR OF THE REAL LIFE

1. Design that combines drawings and lettering. From the Kulte company.

2-3-4-5-6. Illustrations of motorcycles and cars, with colors and retro typography, used for children's T-shirts.

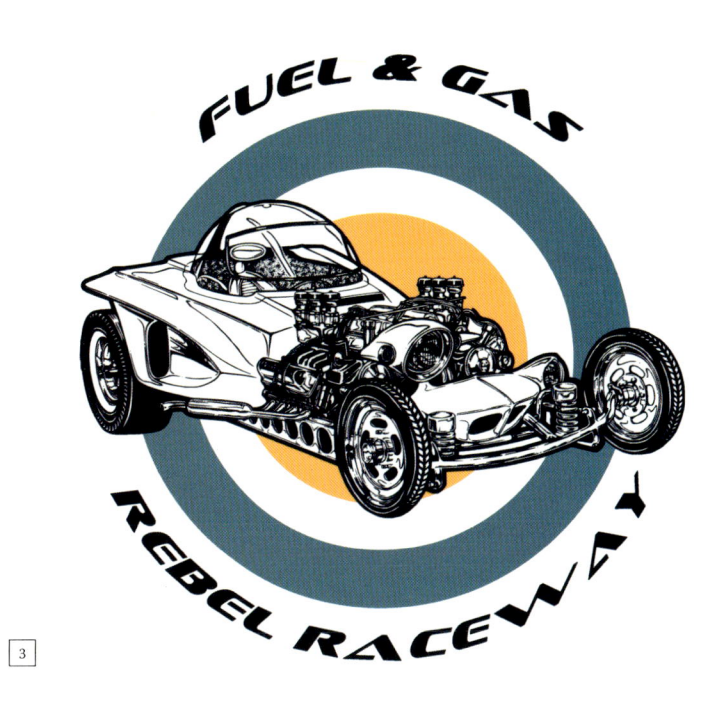

sport life **151**

FAIRY TALES
STORIES AND FABLES

Fairy tales and fables spring from worlds created by imagination and tradition. Fairies, elves, trolls, giants, and even witches and demons constitute the regular cast of characters of these narratives, which frequently have their origin in folklore and are represented in designs within the aesthetic influences of every period.

Although they are most often found on baby and children's clothing, the imaginative motifs, inspired by these fabulous stories and full of color, appear on prints of very diverse style.

Drawings for T-shirts inspired by fables (WGSN).

fairy tales 153

1

2

1. Positional print for a girl's T-shirt that displays record covers from the 1970s.

2. Design for children's wear reflecting a 50-year-old retro aesthetic.

3

4

154 STYLES AND MOTIFS: gallery

3-4-5-6. Illustrations for children's clothing based on cartoons.

7-8. Designs inspired by candy wrappers; children's advertizing from the 1950s. By Laura Fernández.

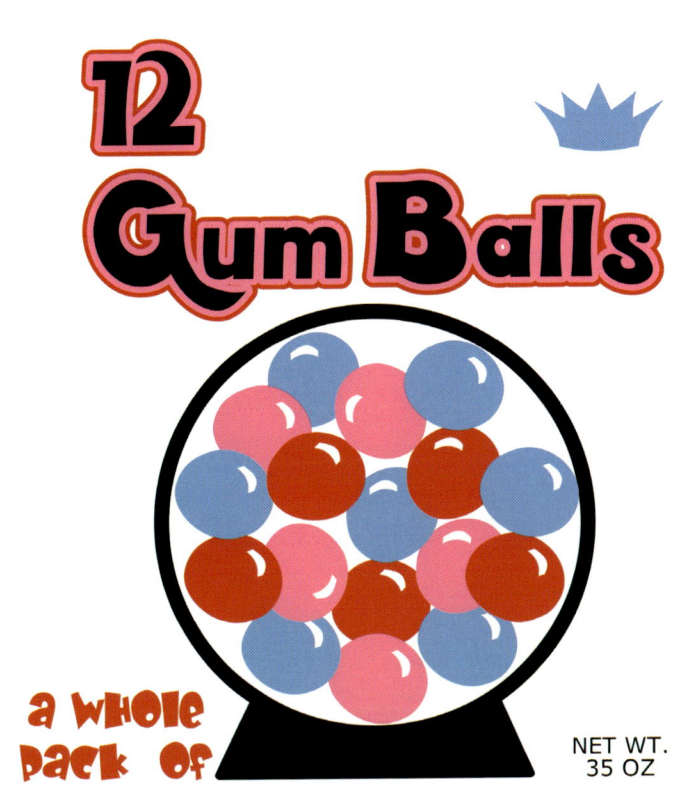

fairy tales **155**

156 STYLES AND MOTIFS: gallery

1-2. Simple-line and naive motifs in design. From the La Casita de Wendy company.

3-4-5-6-7. Continuous prints for textiles for children's clothing. By Aimée Wilder.

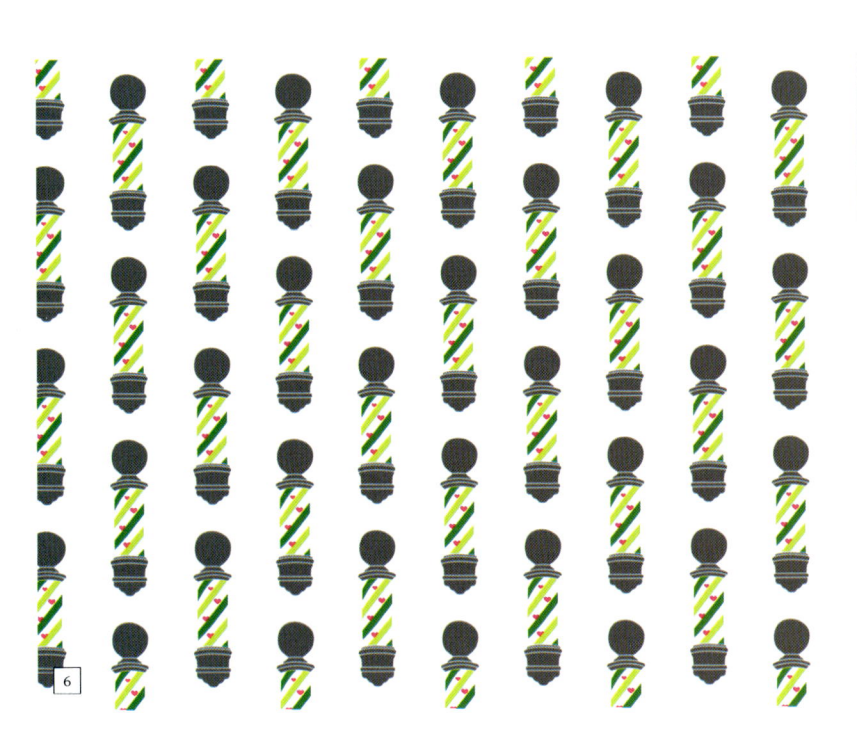

fairy tales **157**

NOAH'S ARK
REAL OR IMAGINARY ANIMALS

In the short stories known as fables, there is a multitude of characters, almost always animals, that exhibit human characteristics. Illustrations of these characters frequently appear on children's clothes. They include animals with attitudes, colors, and fantastical shapes that are shown in drawings intended to stimulate the imagination of even small toddlers. Even in the adult world, animals often symbolize heroic, exotic, or perhaps rustic themes.

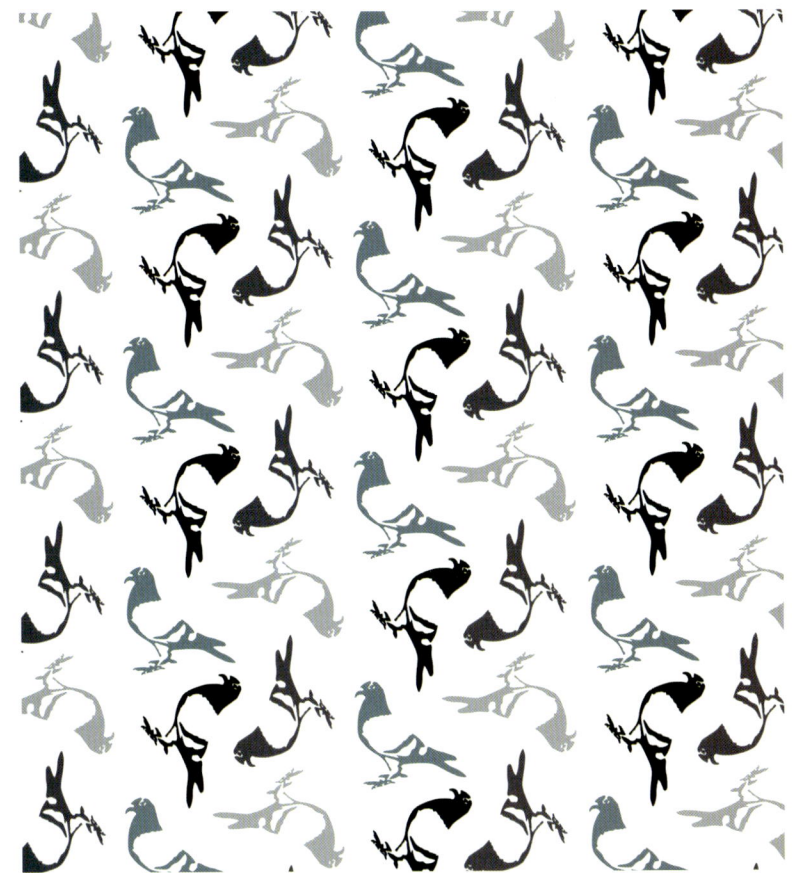

Animal figures for continuous prints. By Aimée Wilder.

160 STYLES AND MOTIFES: gallery

1-2-3-4. Animal skins and feathers reproduced in an almost photographic way (WGSN).

5-6-7-8. Continuous prints from the animal silhouettes (WGSN).

noah's ark **161**

162 STYLES AND MOTIFES: gallery

1-2-3-4-5. Positional designs of animal themes focused on a juvenile clientele (WGSN).

6-7-8. Positional prints for children's clothes (WGSN).

noah's ark **163**

164 STYLES AND MOTIFES: gallery

1-2. T-shirts printed for the Perros collection from the Divinas Palabras company. Spring-Summer collection 2005.

3-4-5. Designs from the Loros series, *Parrots, Bats & Insects*. By Laura Fernández for the company Giulio. Fall-Winter 08/09 collection.

noah's ark **165**

EXOTIC TRIPS
ASIA, AFRICA, SOUTH AMERICA

Exoticism is a taste for that which is foreign. It is the search for the unusual, for images that transport you to different worlds, and it's fed by the imagination and a sense of adventure. Thriving on images of remote lands and different times, this motif transports the spirit to imaginary scenarios that appeal to the instinct for exploration—a taste for what is unusual and distinct. Prints of ethnic inspiration are frequently based on the rich iconography of Africa, Asia, and South America. With these themes, year after year, catwalks present landscapes, scenes of daily life, and abstract designs that refer to forms and colors that are part of these cultures. And, after passing through the eye of the contemporary designer, they are revitalized in intense prints.

1. Hawaiian-inspired design. By Aimée Wilder.

2-3-4-5. Drawings of tropical flowers. By Laura Fernández for the Xbaby and Massimo Dutti companys.

exotic trips **167**

168 STYLES AND MOTIFES: gallery

2-3. Prints inspired by arabesque calligraphy. By Sisters Gulassa.

1-4-5. Forms and colors that reflect Asian cultures (WGSN).

exotic trips **169**

1. Vectorial design for embroidery for the back and front of a hooded sweatshirt. By Inocuo The Sign for the Artful Dodger company.

2. Composition inspired by the London of 1800. Cutter Lads collection. From the Artful Dodger company.

3. Exotic figures in positional drawing. Trip collection. From the Artful Dodger company.

4. Composition of drawings done by hand. From the Artful Dodger company.

170 STYLES AND MOTIFES: gallery

Drawings for a collection inspired by the hallucinations of 19th century travellers affected by unknown illnesses. From the Artful Dodger company.

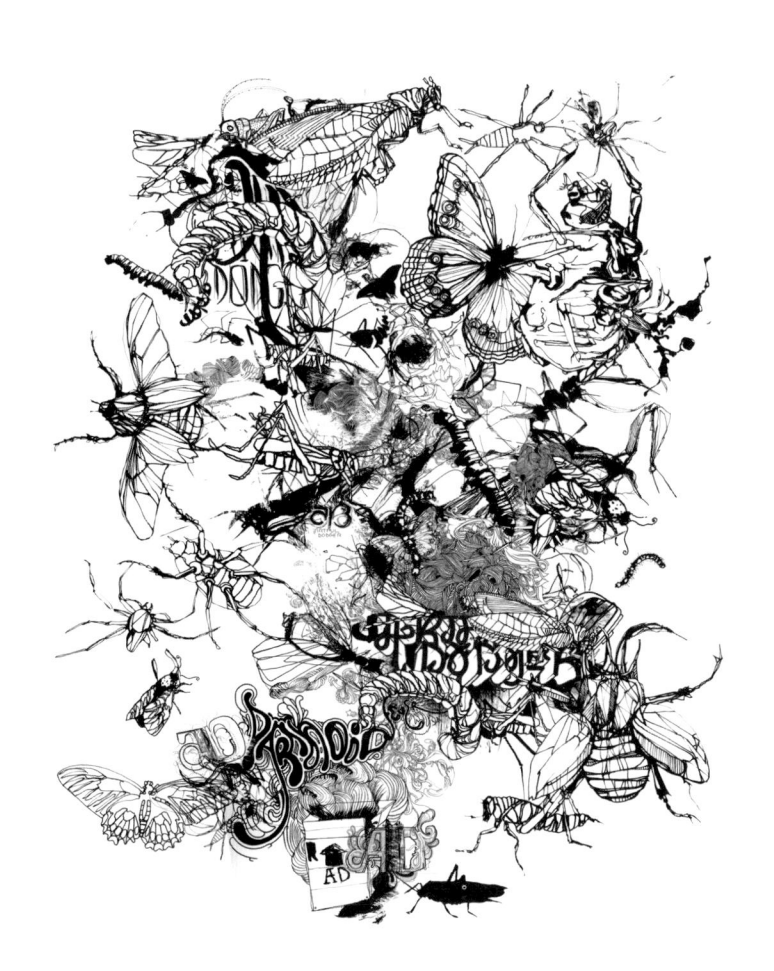

exotic trips 171

TYPOGRAPHY
LETTERS AND NUMBERS, IDEAS AND MESSAGES

Typography plays a foundational role as a source of inspiration. This mode of expression reached its high point with conceptual art, which reappeared with ferocity at the end of the 1980s and was sometimes manifested in phrases transmitted electronically.

The type size and the way the characters are used reinforce the message the designer wants to transmit. Calligraphic ornaments, whose origins go back to very early cultures, play a key role in this technique.

172 STYLES AND MOTIFES: gallery

[2]

[3]

1. Illustration New World. Hombre versus máquina collection. From the Artful Dodger company.

2. Illustration for T-shirt.

3. Inscription Blood Sweat and Silk for sweatshirt.

4. Logo for T-shirt.

5. Logos for back part of sweatshirt. 1835 Collection. From the Industrial Revolution company.

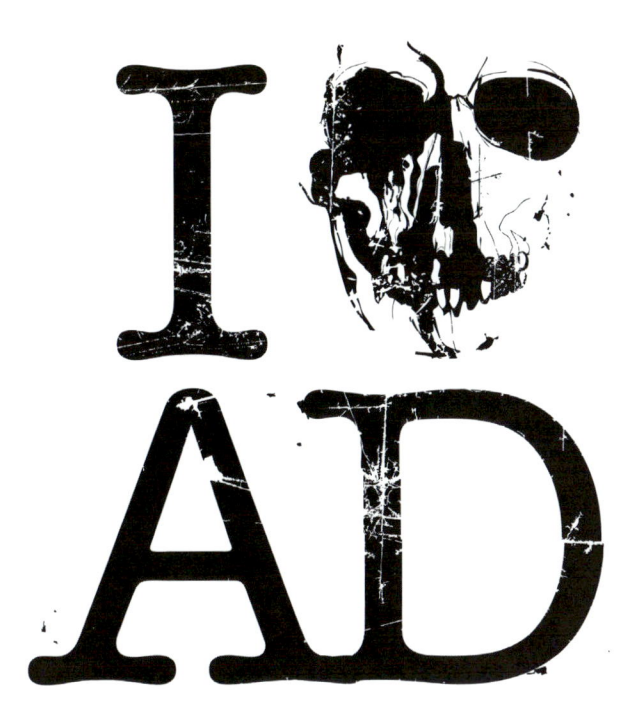

[4]

[5]

letters and numbers **173**

1-2-3-4-5-6. The meaning of the words is reflected in the typefaces that are created for every design (WGSN).

7-8-9-10. Illustrations for screenprinted T-shirts (WGSN).

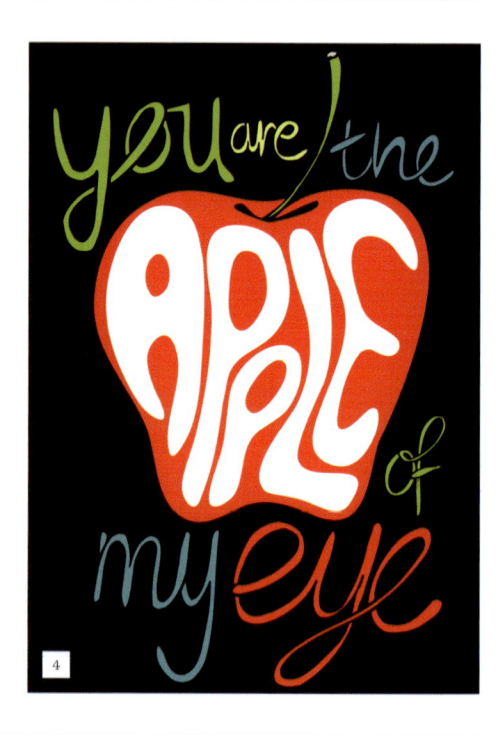

174 STYLES AND MOTIFES: gallery

7

8

9

10

letters and numbers **175**

Une petite maison dans les nuages, une petite fleur quand il pleut l'herbe lui sert de paravent, l'oiseau sur la branche vient de s'envoler, un petit amour dans mon coeur, pour toujours...

1

1. Design that uses French as a language to highlight romanticism.

2. Design with foliage pattern that reinforces the romantic nature of the message.

3. Combination of letters and flowers used to illustrate a woman's T-shirt.

4. Flowers & Skulls design that combines typography with objects.

176 STYLES AND MOTIFES: gallery

Lovely To See You

fleur du paradis

Si il est une
fleur au paradis
qu'elle se penche
sur le terre

Bad girls can be nice

letters and numbers **177**

ART
FROM BAROQUE TO BAUHAUS AND THE ABSTRACT

Art and fashion have always been historically linked. But, although both disciplines interact and are recognized as interpreters of their time, normally, it is fashion designers that transfer the world of painting to their creations. From the influence of Japanese art in the prints of mid-19th century to Art Nouveau style at the beginning of the 20th, through the rationalism of the Bauhaus, the ironies of Pop Art, and the simpleness of Minimalism, clothes can be recognized as a mobile canvas. The most sublime example of this is the iconic dress in the Autumn 1965 collection of Yves Saint Laurent, which reproduced the geometrical compositions of Piet Mondrian. Architecture, also immediately linked to art, has been connected more than ever to fashion in the last few years thanks to profound changes in the materials and construction techniques available.

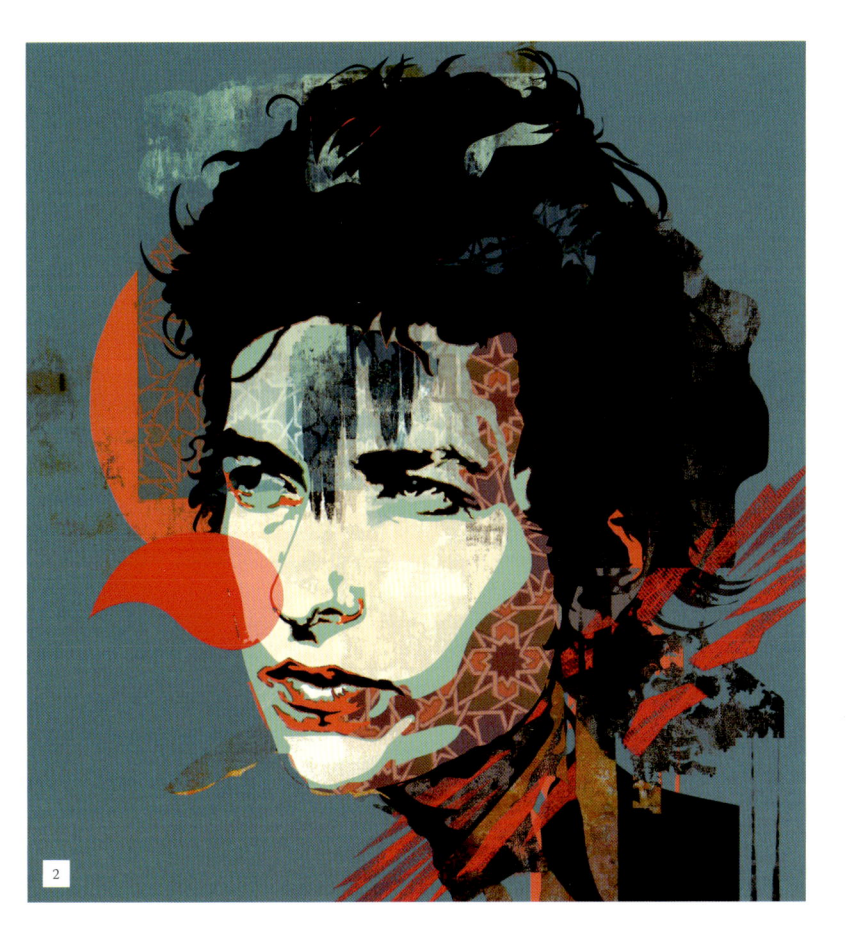

1. Forms and colors that refer to the Pop Art movement. From the Sisters Gulassa company.

2. Image of Bob Dylan for positional print that takes on the same aesthetics as Pop Art (WSGN).

3-4. Portraits that recur in various pictorial techniques of the 20th century (WSGN).

art 179

180 STYLES AND MOTIFES: gallery

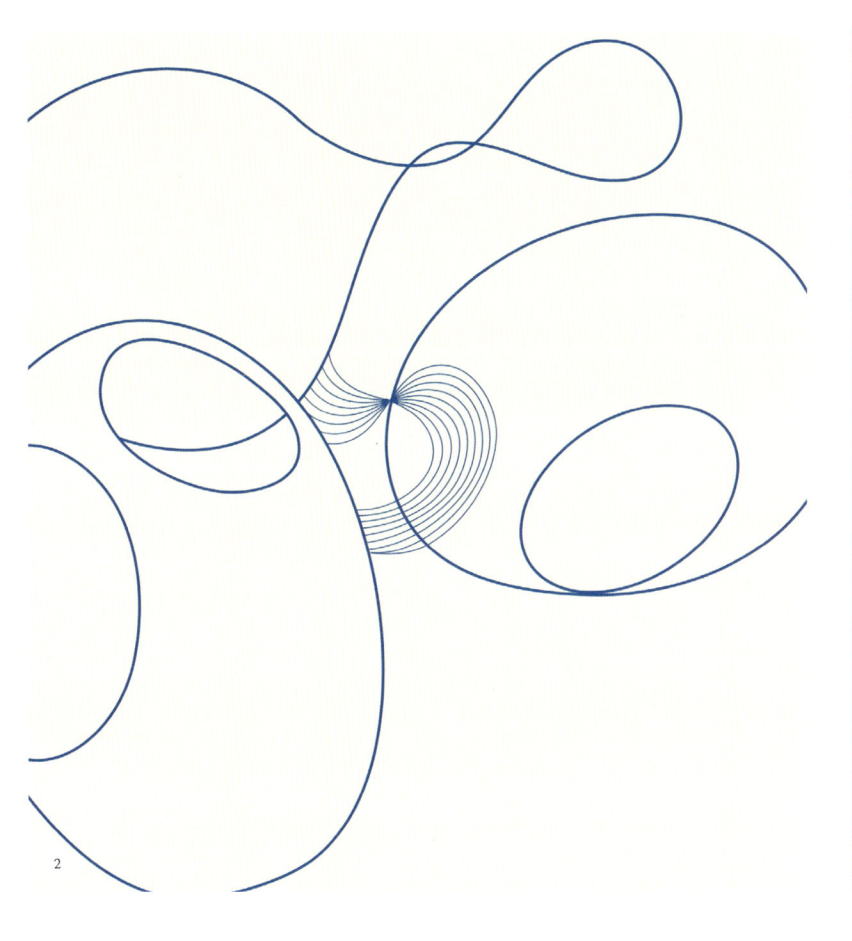

1-2-3. Illustrations inspired by the optical art (Op Art) of the 1960s (WGSN).

4. Illustration in the Art Deco style (WGSN).

art **181**

1

182 STYLES AND MOTIFES: gallery

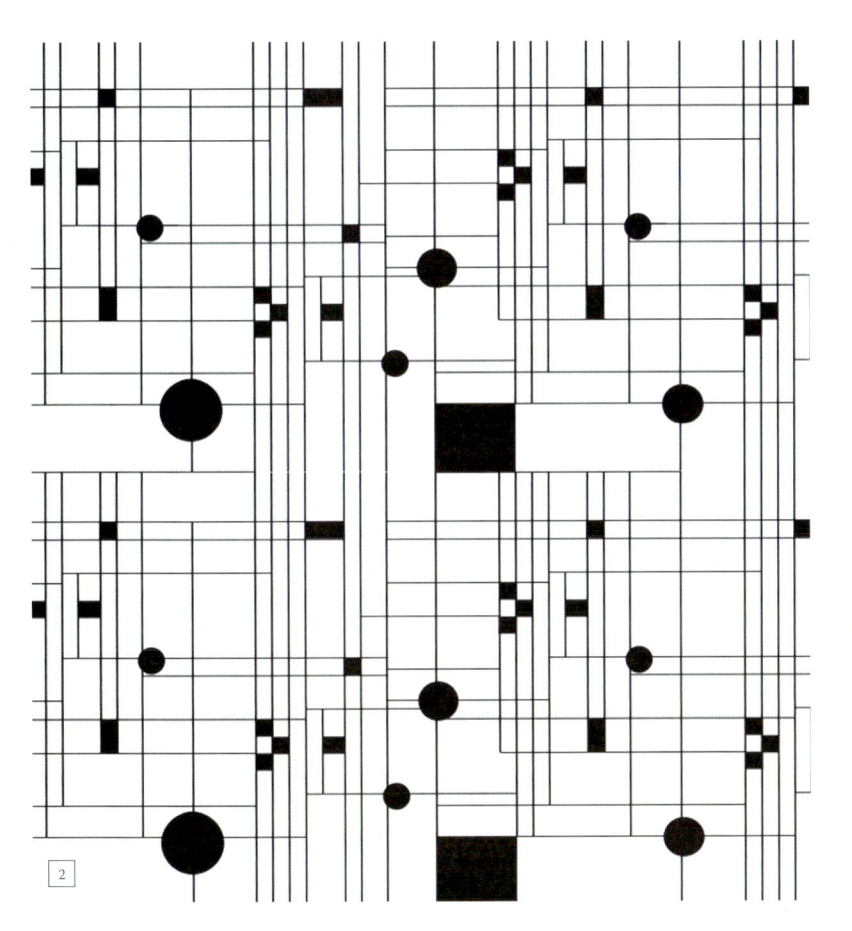

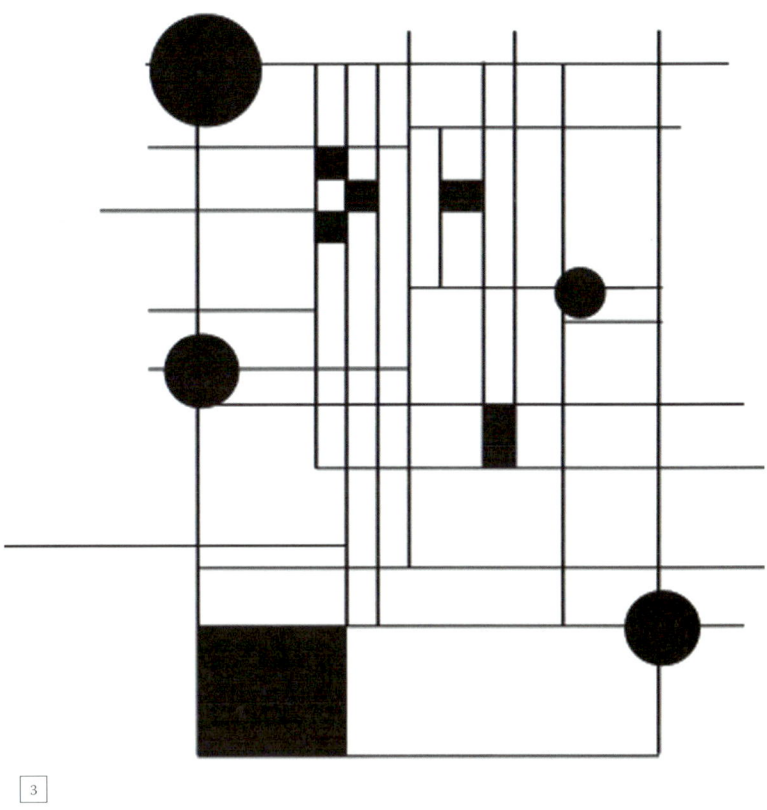

1. Abstract composition that reflects the aesthetics of the vanguards of the first half of the 20th century (WGSN).

2-3-4-5. Prints inspired by the symmetry and the technical rationality of Bauhaus. By Laura Fernández for the Giulio company. Winter 2008/2009 collection.

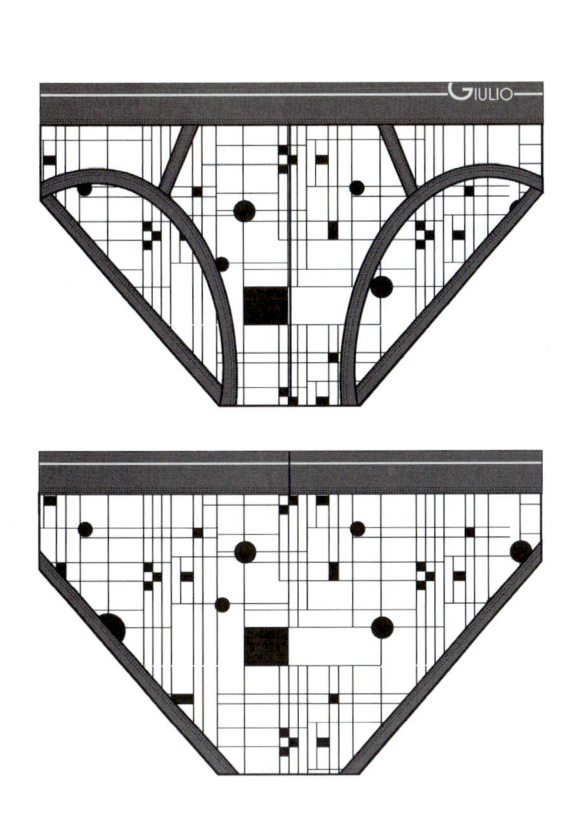

art 183

184 STYLES AND MOTIFES: gallery

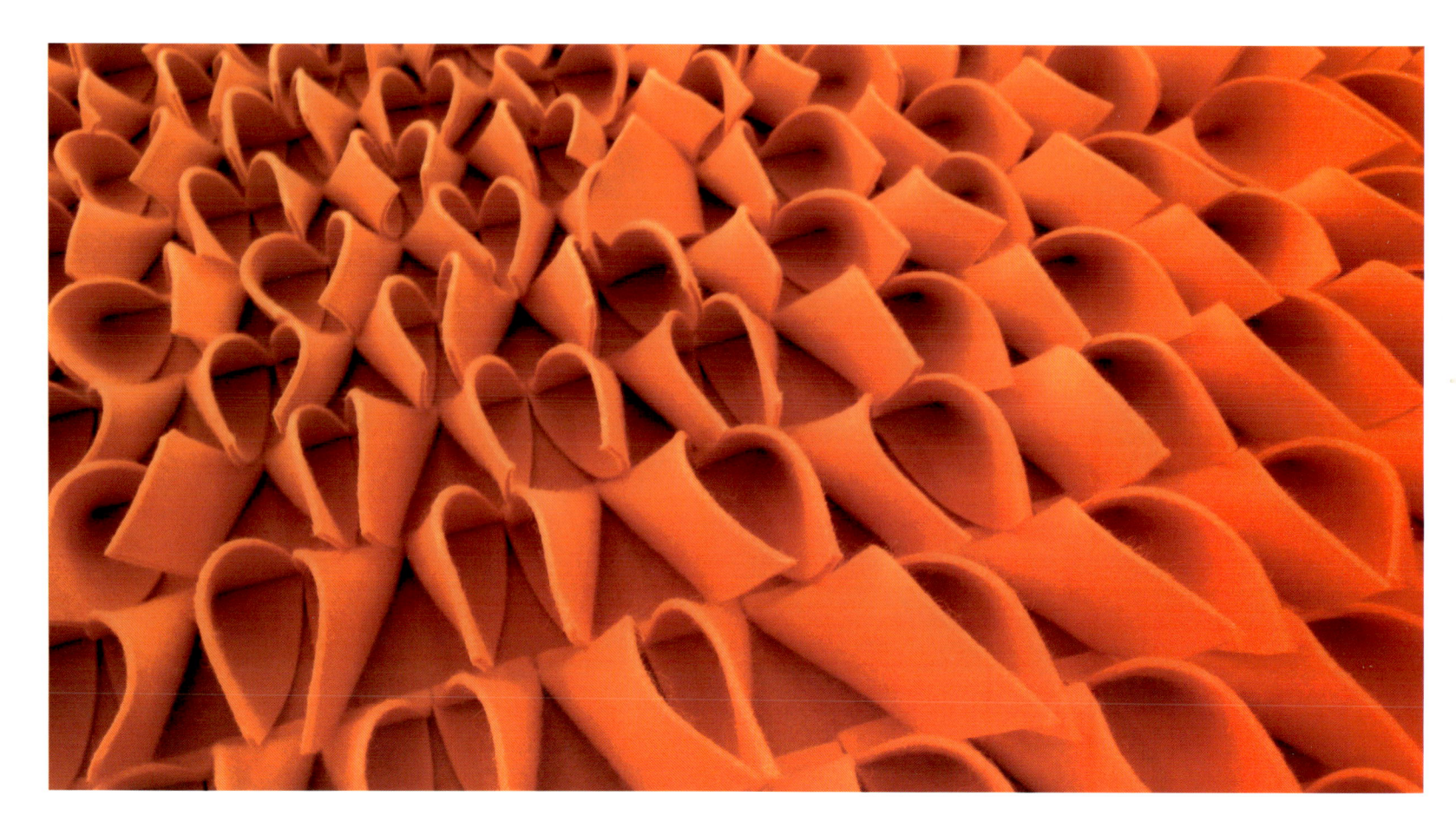

The textile designer Anne Kyyrö Quinn works with forms, volumes, and textures with an almost architectonic construction.

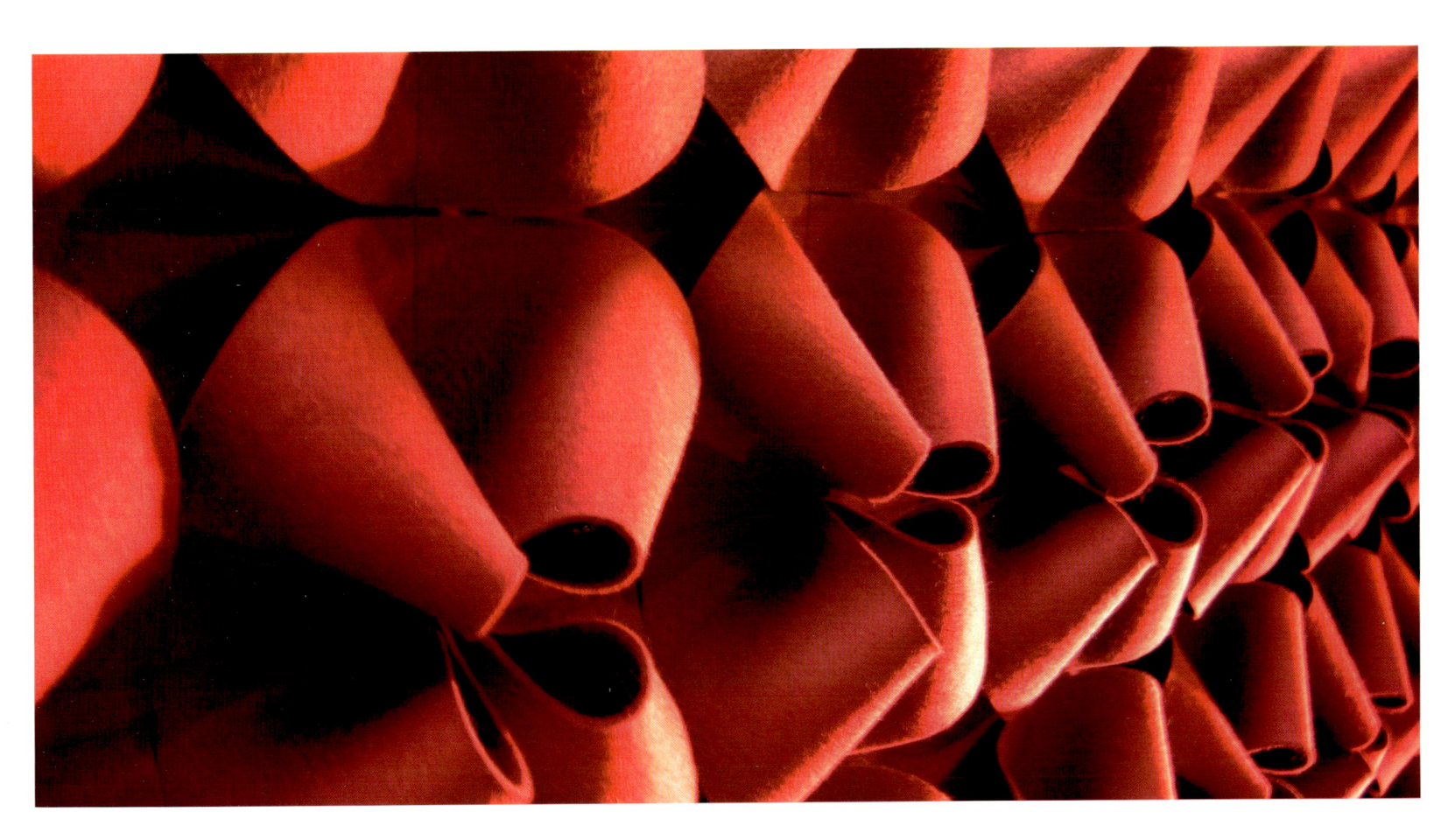

NEW ROMANTIC
DESIGNS FROM THE IMAGINATION

The origin of ornamental motifs is rooted in the symbols of various cultures from down on through the centuries. Rococo, Baroque, Classicism, Islamic, Gothic, and Romanesque are only some examples of the styles that gave life to forms inspired by nature and by sublimating ancestral cultural symbols until eventually generating images of extreme beauty. In many cases, these designs even have their origin in the spiritual plane (such as the yin and yang in Asian culture or the sinuous forms of the Celtic culture).

1. Digital, positional design for the neckline of a dress. By Laura Fernández.

2-3. Prints that reflect the iconography of death in Mexico. From the Mátala Mamá company.

4-5. Prototypes of positional prints for T-shirts. By Laura Fernández for Springfield. Fall-Winter 2005/2006 collection.

ornamental **187**

1. Original print with the slogan Rock & Circus. Spring-Summer 2006 collection. From the Mátala Mamá company.

2. Inspiration for the Art Nouveau women's Autumn-Winter 2005/2006 collection. From the Springfield company.

3-4. Prototypes of positional patterns to t-shirts. Autumn-Winter 2005/2006 collection. From the Springfield company.

5. Composition of musical and floral elements where the stamens are converted into microphones and musical notes are flowers. By Basso & Brooke.

ornamental 189

DIRECTORY

AILANTO
Diputación, 248, 3º
08007 Barcelona, Spain
T. + 34 93 487 06 96
ailanto@ailanto.com
www.ailanto.com

AIMEÉ WILDER
Brooklyn, NY 11211
info@aimeewilder.com
www.aimeewilder.com

ANNE KYYRÖ QUINN
2.06 Oxo Tower Wharf
Bargehouse St, London SE1 9PH, UK
T. + 44 (0)20 7021 0702
info@annekyyroquinn.com
www.annekyyroquinn.com

ATELIER LZC
2, rue M. Berthelot
93100 Montreuil, France
T. + 33 (0)1 42 87 81 34
celine@atelierlzc.fr
www.atelierlzc.fr

BASSO & BROOKE
Via Donizetti, 48
20122 Milan, Italy
T. + 39 02 760 591
francesca.bianco@aeffe.com
www.bassoandbrooke.com

CADENA, S.A.
Río Rosas, 3-5
28003 Madrid, Spain
T. + 34 91 442 60 22
cadena@cadena-sa.com
www.cadena-sa.com

CHRISTIAN DIOR
Monsieur Philippe Le Moult
11 bis, rue François 1er
75008 Paris, France
www.dior.com

DIVINAS PALABRAS
Rambla del Raval, 2 bis, 1º 2ª
08001 Barcelona, Spain
T. + 34 93 562 02 11
info@divinaspalabras.com
www.divinaspalabras.com

GIULIO UNDERWEAR
P. Til·lers, 3-7, 08390 Montgat
Barcelona, Spain
T. + 34 933 892 812
info@giulio.es
www.giulio.es

HAMISH MORROW
contact@hamishmorrow.com
www.hamishmorrow.com

HANNA WERNING - SPRING STREET STUDIO AB
Drottninggatan, 88D 1tr
SE-111 36 Stockholm, Sweden
T. + 46 (0)70 236 57 25
hello@byhanna.com
www.byhanna.com

INOCUO THE SIGN STUDIO
Ciutat de Granada, 28 bis, 4 planta.
08005 Barcelona, Spain
T. + 34 93 45 031 067
hello@inocuothesign.com
www.inocuothesign.com

IVANA HELSINKI
Hämeentie, 157, 5ª planta
FI-00560 Helsinki, Finland
T. + 358-50-347 6131
pirjo@ivanahelsinki.com
www.ivanahelsinki.com

JAVIER NANCLARES
T: + 44 2086743967
j_nanclares@hotmail.com

JAVIER SIMORRA
Pol. Industrial Can Casablancas
Vallès, 3, Sant Quirze del Vallès
08192 Barcelona, Spain
T. + 34 93 721 7978
simorra@simorra.com
www.javiersimorra.com

JOSEP FONT
Ciutat de Granada, 96-98 bajos
08018 Barcelona, Spain
T. + 34 93 300 31 11
Gabriela@josepfont.com
www.josepfont.com

LA CASITA DE WENDY
C/ Nuria, 32, 2º B
28034 Madrid, Spain
T. + 34 91 702 57 85
info@lacasitadewendy.com
www.lacasitadewendy.com

LAURA FERNÁNDEZ
olivia.superstar@gmail.com
http://ladyf-f.blogspot.com
Ligia Unanue Design Studio
C/Rosalía de Castro, 59, bajos
08025 Barcelona, Spain
T.+ 34 93 535 05 00
nurligia@yahoo.es

LOUIS FERAUD
2, rue de Bassano
75116 Paris, France
T.+33 (0)1 49 52 44 00
contact@feraud.com
www.feraud.com

MANUEL ALBARRÁN
artmanuelalbarran@gmail.com
www.manuelalbarran.com

MARCUS JAMES
6, Compton Terrace
London N1 2UN, UK
T: + 07779 099 047
marcus@marcusjames.co.uk
www.marcusjames.co.uk

MARÍA JOSÉ LLEONAR
T: + 34 679 389 792
pepalleonar50@gmail.com

MIRIAM OCÁRIZ
Ribera de Axpe, 11B-L005
Erandio-Vizcaya, Spain
T. + 34 94 475 14 57
info@miriamocariz.com
www.miriamocariz.com

PREMIÈRE VISION PARIS
www.premierevision.fr

RAFA MOLLAR
C/ Arretes, 24-30, local 13
08001 Barcelona, Spain
contacto@rafamollar.com
www.rafamollar.com

SISTERS GULASSA
Backenbrunnlg. 9
1180 Vienna, Austria
T. + 431 470 2490
cyrille@sistersgulassa.com
www.sistersgulassa.com

SHARON WAUCHOB
9, rue de Beauce
75003 Paris, France
T. + 33 1 42776734
contact@sharonwauchob.com
www.sharonwauchob.com

STAR – STAMPA TESSUTI ARTISTICI S.P.A.
via c. Dominioni, 2
22070 Oltrona s. Mamette 8, Como, Italy
T. + 39 031 3531 5
sales@starco.it
www.star.co.it

SYNGMAN CUCALA
Rambla Catalunya, 112
08008 Barcelona, Spain
http://syngmancucala.blogspot.com

VENTURES DESIGNER-SPORTS
23A, Ballygunge Place
Kolkata – 700019 India
T.+ 91 33 2440 0678/0679
sales@venturesfashion.in
www.venturesfashion.in

WGSN - WORTH GLOBAL STYLE NETWORK
C/ Aribau, 175. 3º 2ª B
08036 Barcelona, Spain
T. + 34 93 414 47 56
www.wgsn.com

XIMENA TOPOLANSKY DESIGN
ximenatop@bytfactory.com
www.seriallover.es

ACKNOWLEDGMENTS

This book would not have been possible without the active collaboration and selflessness of the professionals and businesses that have supported us by sharing their work and experience.

BORDADOS EMILIO DIFUSIÓN, S.L.
Ronda Sant Elm, 37
08360 Canet de Mar. Barcelona
bordados@emiliosdifusion.com
www.emiliosdifusion.com

ESTAMPADOS LICENCIADOS S.L.
Trav. Can Maresme, 9.
Barrio Cotet, 08338 Premià de Dalt. Barcelona, Spain
estampados@terra.es

INDIGO PARIS
info@indigo-salon.com
www.indigo-salon.com

INSTITUT CATALÀ DE LA MODA
Gran Vía, 696. Barcelona, Spain
www.incatmoda.com

KARINA ZARFINO
Textile Design and History of Shoes (Consulting)
T. + 34 667 867 693
karinazarfino@yahoo.es

MARCO PERI FOTOGRAFÍA
marcoperi@gmail.com

NOS & SOTO FOTÒGRAFS
C/ Lepant, 264, 6º D
08013 Barcelona, Spain
T.+ 34 93 2459276

COVER COPYRIGHT
Miriam Ocáriz